HOW TO DEVELOP A LOW-COST FAMILY FOOD-STORAGE SYSTEM

by Anita Evangelista

Breakout Productions
Port Townsend, Washington

How to Develop a Low-Cost
    Family Food-Storage System
© 1995 by Anita Evangelista

Published by:
Breakout Productions
PO Box 1643
Port Townsend, WA 98368

ISBN 0-9666932-0-5
Library of Congress Card Catalog 98-88046

CONTENTS

ACKNOWLEDGEMENTS

Some of the material in this book has appeared in different form in the following excellent publications:

Back Home Magazine

Backwoods Home Magazine

Fine Gardening Magazine

Maine Organic Farmer & Gardener

Small Farmer's Journal

The Sheep Producer

ONE:
WHY STORE FOOD?

This is a question which could only be asked in a Western nation during the latter twentieth century, oddly enough. In the "Third World" and in our country in *all* centuries prior to this one, individuals, families, and communities stored excess foods. For instance, archeological digs in 2,000-year-old Roman villas — the homes of the rich — turn up "amphora." These large pottery jugs, often three feet tall, were capable of holding thirty gallons of liquid or about fifty pounds of grain each. A typical villa might have several hundred amphora in a cellar, providing stored foods for a single family — even though seasonal farmers' markets were the norm in that time... just as supermarkets are the norm in ours.

Ultimately, the thought behind all personal food-storage systems is a sense of *insecurity*. There are people, perhaps the majority of our population, who do not feel this insecurity and simply cannot understand why anyone would want to store foods. Perhaps they are right; perhaps even though history records the horrors of famine through the ages, the rise and fall of civilizations based on insufficient foodstuffs; even though in our own time we can see TV news images of starving peoples, perhaps we are safe in the US.

Of course, these secure people must live in major cities — because the majority of my very rural neighbors routinely store a few foods for winter use. It may be a vestige of the pioneer spirit, or more practical reasons rather than a sense of insecurity, which drive them. After all, country roads do get closed by heavy snowfalls or ice, forcing residents to rely on stored supplies for days or weeks at a stretch. Is it insecurity which compels these country folk to store up, or a simple prudence based on past experience?

Your own reasons for wanting to develop a family food supply may be built on a sense of insecurity, or on a deeper desire for self-sufficiency. But it's helpful to recognize *why* you want to store foods. Here are possible reasons other people have suggested:

1. Severe seasonal weather, with road closures, power outages, and supermarkets depleted by panic buyers.
2. Natural disasters such as earthquakes, tidal waves, hurricanes, volcanoes, or tornadoes, with supermarkets unable to restock shelves.
3. Ecological disasters, such as the Three Mile Island nuclear facility's failure, and contamination of foods.
4. The possibility of nuclear holocaust with all food deliveries suspended.

5. Tainted foodstuffs, either by purposeful maniacs (as in the "pain-killer poisonings") or improper processing (as in the glass fragments found in baby foods, or salmonella bacteria in dairy foods).
6. Riots, civil insurrection, collapse of local or regional governing bodies, gang warfare, looting, racial incidents; inability to shop at all.
7. Long-term illness.
8. Loss of employment and inability to secure a new job.
9. Strikes, either by truckers, food processors, food pickers or supermarket employees.
10. Destruction of standing food crops in farmers' fields, either willfully or by natural calamities.
11. Collapse of the currency system, and inability to purchase needed goods.

Some of these "insecurity-makers" have already happened in the US, including Florida's Hurricane Andrew in 1992, the Loma Prieta California earthquake in 1989, and the 1992 Los Angeles riots. (During December of 1989, my family had a personal mini-disaster, with our roads frozen into slick glaciers — we were literally unable to leave the house for a full month.) Tainted foodstuffs are almost routine in some cities; strange weather patterns destroy food crops every year such as 1993's Gila River flood in Arizona which washed out thousands of acres of winter vegetables. An event doesn't have to be "end of the world" for it to mean "end of the food," at least for a while.

On the other hand, some people prefer the idea of storing food as a positive statement — an affirmation of their preparedness and prudence. Their reasons for keeping up a supply may include:

1. The wholesomeness of home-grown and processed foods.
2. Freshness of stored winter vegetables. (Some varieties are bred especially for long-keeping abilities. See Appendix One.)

3. The ready availability and ease of use of supplies.
4. The variety of foods in storage, ideally suited to the family's tastes.
5. Convenience of having foods on hand for "inspiration" cooking.
6. The frank security of having all you could possibly want to eat easily within reach.
7. The outright thriftiness of storing bulk purchased or homegrown goods — at a fraction of regular prices.
8. The ability to use one's own food production as a method of barter during tough times (such as trading a home-grown ham or fancy liqueur for an automobile's tune-up).
9. The sense of timelessness and attunement to history that storing food provides.
10. Adherence to religious beliefs favored by some groups, such as Latter-Day Saints and Amish.
11. The ability to sleep soundly at night, assured that no matter what happens there will be plenty to eat.

That last point is probably the most important "insecurity-chaser" of all — the absolute assurance of your next meal, that your children and spouse will have enough to eat no matter what. This assurance answers all the fears and concerns of the storage question. It explains to all the doubters why food storage should be undertaken: "Because I'll be confident that we can eat." You can then answer the old saying "Whomever controls your food controls your life," by saying, "I'm in control."

STORING OR HOARDING?

For some people, the idea of food storage is the same as food hoarding. "Hoarding" is perceived as an immoral act of deprivation — stealing or theft of a commodity which is in short supply. To a few individuals, having more food than you need at any one moment is the same as hoarding. Of course, these same folks generally have more shoes than they can wear at one time (that is, more than one pair!), but they don't see this as "shoe hoarding." These same people may have more cash in stocks, bonds and savings accounts than they can spend, but they don't see this as "money hoarding"!

Generally, the idea of "hoarding" only comes into play during crisis situations. And it is only those who have not prepared for the crisis who invoke the word — they failed to store up their own supply, and they're envious of those who actually did. I believe that everyone has the same opportunities to prepare and store foods, RIGHT NOW, that I do... so, I'm not "hoarding" any scarce supplies.

STORING AND BELIEVING

Some, but not all, Bible-believing Christians feel that storing food is an act of "unbelief," a statement of lack of faith in God's provenance. While I can understand this position, I also notice that these same people don't expect God to provide dinner on their table each evening — these people work, buy foods, prepare them, set the table and then sit down to eat. If they trust fully in God's ability to provide, why don't they just sit down and wait for dinner to appear?

Eating isn't a matter of faith. Being protected by God during a crisis isn't a matter of faith — you'll be protected or you won't, by God's will. But if part of your own or your family's survival depends on you heeding God's advance warnings — and then preparing — isn't it an act of unbelief to deny those warnings?

THE PURPOSE OF THIS BOOK

Developing a personal food-storage system can be quite a difficult undertaking, particularly if you have not given the subject much previous consideration — after all, most of us are accustomed to having a supermarket right around the corner. It was only as I was trying to supply my family's needs that I realized very few good systems had been developed which fit our true situation.

Throughout this book, I'll be drawing upon the accumulated food-storage wisdom of a number of different philosophies. This includes the wheat-based Mormon system; the back-to-the-land grow-your-own concept; the organic-only approach; the greenhouse system; and a few others. Each of these concepts has some useful ideas, but I believe most of the approaches previously developed are too steeped in philosophical considerations to realistically address a food-storage situation.

Let me give you an example: When my family was ice-bound for almost a month, we had plenty to eat. I'd stored garden produce, supermarket goods, and assorted other necessities (toilet paper, thank goodness). But I had failed to consider the psychological aspects of being stuck in a mini-disaster, as do virtually all other approaches to food storage.

After the second week, with no end to the freeze in sight, I began to crave soda pop — not something we usually consumed, anyway. Then both kids started to ask for potato chips, another "special occasion" food that wasn't in our pantry. No food-storage system I'd heard of ever included those items, or candy, or popcorn, or other "junk" foods that we often associate with fun or good times. Certainly, these foods weren't necessary for our survival or even for our health — but the emotionally-depressed mood that went with being trapped at home would have been considerably lightened by a chocolate bar, or a beer, at an opportune moment.

I cannot imagine a more dreary diet than one based almost entirely on foods made from wheat, no matter how nutritious it is. I cannot conceive of a more difficult diet than one composed of dehydrated foodstuffs with which I am unfamiliar. You know how difficult it is to get kids or old folks to eat unfamiliar foods — imagine trying to force "gluten burgers" or "reconstituted chili" on freaked-out youngsters while the wind howls or the earth shakes!

As all good cooks know, there's more to eating than simply "refueling the machine." Satisfying eating relies on taste, color, texture and fragrance, not just sufficient calories. In a time of crisis, you'll thank yourself a thousand times for the familiar foods you've stored up — and a million times for the treats!

THE RULES OF FOOD STORAGE

So I have developed several rules of thumb for our own food storage system, which undoubtedly will apply to your own approach:

Supreme Rule: Do not tell *anyone* that you have stored up foods. Not anyone. Especially acquaintances. The main reason is that most people will believe you've gone completely paranoid and try to talk you out of it. The second reason is that during a time of crisis, your name will be the first one people think of... and uninvited guests are not a desirable situation during a crisis.

Rule One: Store foods which you regularly eat, and eat the foods which you store; this keeps your supply fresh and familiar. One of our most unpleasant stored-food experiences was trying to eat a variety of freeze-dried carrot. The flavor was weird, the texture unsatisfying, no matter how it was prepared. I'm glad our main food supply was familiar stuff.

Rule Two: Store more than you think you will need, in case extra relatives or friends become dependent on you; and to allow for spoilage.

Rule Three: Store some "fun foods" — hard candy, soda, drinks, etc. — because if you're in a tough situation, you'll really want the relief they provide.

Rule Four: Store *at least* two week's supply of pet food at all times. You will not want to see your dog or cat hungry during a crisis, and your pet will become a terrible nuisance if it is not fed according to routines. A domestic animal cannot fend for itself during a crisis, any more than children can. The same goes for livestock.

Rule Five: Rotate your stored foods, either with a definite plan or by using old items before new ones.

Rule Six: Always serve at least one fresh food with each meal — garden or planter-grown lettuce, sprouts, or even a crisp carrot salad fits the bill. This supplies vital nutrients.

Rule Seven: Include a supply of multi-vitamins with your storage program, and make sure each family member takes theirs according to schedule. During a crisis, your body uses its own store of vitamins at a more rapid rate — you'll need the additional supply to maintain optimum health.

Rule Eight: Every now and then, go and take a long, hard, serious look at your food storage supply — and congratulate yourself on your prudence, preparedness and thrift. It takes commitment, planning, wise shopping, extra gardening and plain old organization to carry off a food-storage program, and you should appreciate all the effort that has gone into it!

TWO:
HOW TO DETERMINE
YOUR FOOD-STORAGE NEEDS

There are dehydrated or freeze-dried food-storage plans that consist of rather unique meals designed to fit some sort of "ideal" eater. They allow 2,100 calories per day, per consumer, of luscious menus including "beef bourguignon" or "chicken à la king".

Unfortunately, my husband, who does a great deal of physical labor, will lose weight on less than 4,000 calories daily; and my kids don't think they've eaten if potatoes aren't included somewhere on their plates. And I've got to have at least five cups of strong coffee every day (a bad habit, I know, but that's the way it is). So while those "idealized" storage programs *are* very handy, easy to store, portable, and readily fixable, they simply won't fit our true needs.

Furthermore, most of the dehydrated "complete" menu programs are much more expensive than my paltry budget will allow. (If I could, though, I'd definitely include nitrogen-packed flour, rice and pasta from one of these programs. We use those products, and the long-term packaging would be ideal.)

The truth is, my family eats differently than anybody else's. So do you and yours. You may have higher needs for meats in your diet, or a greater demand for fresh vegetables, or a particular dislike for some foods (turnips, broccoli, asparagus, sauerkraut, etc.) that are favorites in mine. Your family's needs must become the very basis for your food-storage program, because whatever you store is what you will have to eat.

WHAT YOU EAT

I truly had no idea of our routine food consumption until I began doing two things: I saved cash register receipts from supermarket shopping for two weeks, and I wrote down daily menus for the same period of time. Some readers may already do this, but for me it was a new experience to discover the amazing amounts of some products we consumed.

For instance, we regularly ate about twenty pounds of potatoes during a two-week period. Two pounds of peanut butter and six loaves of bread might disappear, as well. We consumed about fourteen pounds of pasta, three pounds of rice and a good twelve pounds of meat. Half a gallon of oil or shortening would go, as well as two pounds of butter. Four pounds of various dried beans went, along with five pounds of carrots. Two pounds of coffee were consumed, plus small quantities of various other items.

Get the picture? A great deal more food than I realized was swallowed up by my four-person (two adult, two teenager) family.

This two-week record of our eating habits taught me the importance of our own personal food storage: no other system I'd ever heard of included *that much* meat, oil, or potatoes.

This record also gave me a pretty good idea of how much food we'd need to store for a full week's diet — and by multiplying the two-week menu by two, I had a complete month's diet.

If I wanted to store three months' worth of food, I would multiply the two-week amount by six.

If I preferred a six-month store, I should multiply by twelve.

A STORAGE PROGRAM FOR ONE MONTH

I have looked through my records and put together a complete listing for a single month's food needs for my four-person family. This listing can provide you with some ideas for your own use, but really shouldn't be used directly as a guide for your food storage.

These are our basics for an ordinary month:

20 quarts of meat (about 40 pounds)
15 quarts of potatoes (40 pounds)
15 pounds dried beans
15 pounds dried pasta
15 pounds rice
60 quarts mixed fruit (90 pounds)
8 ½ gallons of milk
12 loaves of bread
15 pounds flour
60 quarts cooked or fresh vegetables including tomatoes
6 quarts sauerkraut

8 pounds butter
1 gallon shortening
8 dozen eggs
4 pounds coffee
5 pounds oatmeal
4 boxes corn flakes
4 pounds cheese
2 pounds corn meal
1 pound salt
3 pounds sugar or honey
6 heads of lettuce or other fresh greens

Extras: yeast, baking powder, pepper, garlic, seasonings, bouillon cubes, cornstarch, raisins, nuts, popcorn, hard candy, cocoa powder, yogurt, buttermilk, pickles, herb teas, gelatin, vinegar.

With these supplies on hand, I could fix any kind of meal we are familiar with — plus whip up special fixin's to suit a spur-of-the-moment inspiration, such as oatmeal cookies or chocolate cake. Cooking foods pretty much from scratch is, naturally, the least-expensive way to put meals together — plus, it allows numerous combinations of basic ingredients to prepare new dishes from published recipes. But I wouldn't hesitate to keep packaged mixes if that's what I ordinarily used.

We could probably include another small family in our meals several times (though not for the full month) with this list. We'd all have plenty to eat, too.

Personally, a complete one-month supply of stored foods is the absolute minimum I am comfortable with. If you have never stored foods, I'd suggest aiming for a two-week supply — that will seem like an exorbitant amount initially. After you have been storing foods for a while, you can expand quite quickly to a one-month supply. Then, on to three months' worth — and, if you want, a full year's complement of foodstuffs.

But for starters, make your two-week list of foods your family consumes. If you are really determined to store up, include sundries (shampoo, toilet paper, shavers, etc.) for an accurate picture of your consumption patterns. The next chapter explains how to build up your supply of the foods you use.

THREE:
LOW-COST SOURCES
FOR YOUR FOODS

The chapter is about acquiring a sturdy food supply without depleting your money supply. Since nothing is free, it follows that if you truly want a LOW-COST food storage system, you must trade time for dollars — putting in effort instead of bucks. The low-cost food sources that follow are all dependent on the application of *time* and *energy* to complete, two things most of us have. If you have a lack of either time or energy, then dollars can take their place. But I'll assume you'd prefer to spend your hard-earned money as efficiently as possible, trading time and energy whenever you can.

The low-cost sources for foods are out there, mostly invisible. They are: gardening; backyard livestock; bulk buying; "buddy" buying; barter; foraging and hunting; and gleaning. The rest of this chapter includes the benefits and drawbacks of each approach, so that you can explore any one of them with your eyes open.

GARDENING

The single most effective, efficient and inexpensive way to gather a food supply is to grow it. This is true even if you don't have a country residence, and even if you live on a suburban lot or in a city apartment. My first city garden was six feet by eight feet, and produced more lettuce, cherry tomatoes, peppers and sugar snap peas than we could eat. It helped decrease our regular food bill and there was some left for canning and freezing.

Various calculations have been made in the past decade that a 25'x25' garden that was continuously succession-planted and harvested through an ordinary season could "earn" (save) well over a thousand dollars in food costs.

Right now, I have three garden spots: one is 40'x70'; another is 20'x50'; the last is an odd shaped 50'x50'. Between these three areas, I expect to grow about $4,000 worth of food — I know for sure, because that is what I spent for foods two years ago, before the garden plots were in heavy use. As a direct result, I won't have to spend that money on foods this year... which is good since I don't seem to have it!

Quantity gardening is not much more difficult than growing a small patch of foods, but it requires a different mindset and attendance to harvest times. All the ins and outs of growing food are too detailed to cover here; there are many fine books at your local library which detail the subject (see the list at end of this booklet). If you have never gardened before, please don't start too large. A small, highly-productive garden will earn more food than a large weed-covered and neglected patch.

For first time gardeners, the following plants will swamp you with vegetables: six tomatoes, four zucchini, four cucumbers, small row of lettuce, small row of radishes. If you bought seeds for these in the small packets supermarkets sell, you'd spend about $6, and have plenty of seeds left over.

One tomato plant will provide your fresh use, and the fruit of the other three can be canned for later use. The zucchini will overwhelm you right from the start, so be prepared to freeze, can and dry the excess. Use the cucumbers in salads and pickle the extras (these make lovely Christmas gifts). The lettuce and radishes are easy to grow and go right onto the table.

If you plan to grow food organically, consider this option: it takes several years to improve soil to a "purely" organic level. If your goal is to produce food, rather than adhere to ecological philosophy, I'd suggest you begin your soil improvement program the first year, while using chemical-based fertilizers and insecticides sparingly. As you continue to add manure and compost to your soil through the years, you'll have less need for the chemical additives. Organic food tastes and "feels" better, but strictly organic growing won't do you any good if the bugs get your crop first.

Suburban or apartment dwellers who don't have much yard space can use another approach. Purchase inexpensive plastic laundry baskets (generally about $1 each), line them with a trash bag, punch drainage holes in the bottom, and fill with dirt. Soil can be found at construction sites, empty lots, or out of friends' backyards. Include some earthworms, if you can find them. Plant the "beginner's" garden of tomatoes, zucchini, and cukes, at the rate of two plants per basket. Add some marigold seeds to each basket, for prettiness and to deter bugs.

The drawbacks of gardening are very real problems, so don't kid yourself about the apparent easiness of it. You won't be able to produce food unless you genuinely adhere to good gardening practices, and it takes considerable time and effort to learn to garden well. You won't be able to produce all your own food the first year. Fortunately, most people enjoy the mild exercise and close relationship with plants.

Gardening requires tools — at least a digging "fork," trowel, and a hoe for each participant (about $15 per person). Cotton gloves are useful ($2). A small tiller, with its own needs for gas and repairs, makes the work easier. These can sometimes be found used for about $200-300; new tillers may run $800.

The first year, you will have to buy seeds — but if you make sure these are NOT hybrids (that is, "open pollinated," and so will breed true), you can save seeds from your first harvest to plant in succeeding years and cut down future seed costs. If you have to buy manure, fertilizers, or even those bags of "top soil," your costs will climb. Consider keeping small livestock, such as rabbits, to supply this important need. Don't use the poop from your cats or dogs in the garden, though — too much chance of passing their parasites or illnesses on to you.

If you garden, you will have to learn how to preserve your foods as well. This may include canning, drying, salting, pickling, curing or freezing. Each of these has other costs in both time and money associated with them — even though home-grown and processed foods are *still* cheaper than supermarket stuffs. (See the appendix on Methods of Preservation.)

Finally, the biggest drawback to gardening is that you may lose your whole crop. In the cities, "finger blight" (theft) is the main problem; in the country, bugs or weather extremes can cost a portion of your harvest.

BACKYARD LIVESTOCK

If you enjoy eating meat, have a little extra space, and like animals, you can provide for your needs with small livestock. I believe the best stock for home use, even in the suburbs, is domestic rabbit. Second in usefulness is either chickens or coturnix quail.

Rabbits are quiet, clean and easy to care for. I kept over 60 rabbits on a tiny city lot, without neighbors even knowing I had any — and three or four rabbits in cages can pass for "junior's pets." The manure is probably the finest you can find, doesn't have a foul odor, and will not "burn" your plants.

A well-bred meat-type female "doe" rabbit — generally of the New Zealand White or Californian breeds — can supply you with about 130 pounds of rabbit meat yearly in the form of bunnies. She is bred once every three months, and her babies are born about 30 days later. At eight weeks of age, the bunnies should weigh around 4 pounds each and will "dress out" to about two pounds apiece. Two months after giving birth, the doe is rebred and the cycle starts again.

This would work out to about two rabbit dinners per week (a total of four rabbits) for my family, and can replace chicken in most menus. Three females and one male "buck" rabbit can steadily supply almost 400 pounds of meat per year, enough to allow you to eat rabbit almost every day if you want to. (If you don't want to eat that much rabbit, pet shops often are willing to buy healthy extras — or trade them for rabbit food.) The meat is white, very lean to the point of dryness, tender, and tastes milder than chicken.

Rabbit manure can be used straight on the garden, or it can be soaked in water to make "manure tea" plant food. Either way, you won't have to buy additional garden fertilizers.

The drawbacks to rabbit keeping are significant. In some towns, rabbits are considered "farm animals" and you may be visited by irate animal-control authorities who will ask you to remove them. (I've never heard of this happening, though.) Rural residents don't have this concern.

Each rabbit must be kept in a separate cage and supplied with nesting boxes for their babies to be born into. They need waterers and feeders. Young healthy rabbits of breeding age may cost from $3-10 each. A new cage is about $30, nest box $10 and other equipment about $8. However, you can generally find used equipment (be sure to sanitize it first with bleach and thorough rinsing), or you can make cages from 2x4s and heavy wire.

While rabbits enjoy vegetables like carrots and cabbage, they will only produce well for you if you feed them a high-protein (16%-18%) ration. You can make your own from oats, corn, wheat, barley and alfalfa hay — or you can buy alfalfa-based "rabbit pellets" commercial feed. In our area, pellets are about $5 for 50 pounds — about ten days of feed for three does, their twenty-four growing babies, and one buck. In major cities, the feed may cost twice as much. However, that $5 or $10 will provide many pounds of wholesome meat, significantly less expensive than chicken or ground beef. On the average, our rabbits have cost us around thirty-eight cents per pound by the time they get to the table.

Keeping rabbits or other stock means that someone in the family must be responsible for feeding, watering, breeding and managing the health of the animals.

One of the most difficult aspects of raising cute, fuzzy bunnies is butchering day. This is particularly hard if it's your first batch of cuddly babies, and if you have children who have become attached to the animals. It helps if you avoid naming the rabbits, and make pets only of the adult females rather than the babies.

Someone must perform the kill, thumping the animal *hard* on the head with a hammer or stick, then cutting off the head, skinning and gutting it. It is not difficult work physically, and only takes about ten minutes per fryer when you get into it, but it can be very trying for first-timers. It is not financially worthwhile to raise your own rabbits and then pay a butcher to process them — but you might be able to trade several rabbits to a friend who will do the butchering of the rest of them in exchange.

You will also be butchering about eight or so at a time, so you'll need to be prepared to freeze or can the meat within a day or two.

Finally, a drawback which is usually unrecognized is that some rabbits may refuse to breed, or may kill their own young. Predators, too, may kill both bunnies and adult rabbits. Raccoons, cats, opossums, snakes and roaming dogs can't seem to resist rabbit dinners. Extra-heavy cage wire can help prevent predation, and using the uncooperative breeder for stew solves this problem.

Quail and chickens both supply eggs and meat for the home. I've raised both in suburbia and on the farm. Home-produced eggs are deeper yellow in color than supermarket eggs, taste better, and are as fresh as can be. Each adult hen, costing from $3 to $10 apiece, can provide about 280 eggs per year (or more, if from a "laying" variety like Leghorns). If you have a rooster, you can incubate and hatch your next generation for next to nothing, thus supplying meat and more eggs. They can be raised in pens on the ground or in cages like rabbits. Both quail and chickens can be fed commercial feeds, about $5 to $10 per 50 pounds, or can receive ground corn and plenty of greens and access to dirt and bugs. I've heard of Depression-era farmers scraping road-killed animals from the highways to add protein to their chickens' diets.

Coturnix quail are semi-exotic small birds, about the size of a little dove. They are bad-tempered, but incredible producers. The quails begin laying grape-sized speckled eggs when they are only eight weeks old (it takes a chicken about six months to start laying). About five quail eggs equal a large chicken egg in taste and quantity. At the same age, or a little older, the quail are ready for table use. Two baked quail are a single serving and a fancy gourmet treat. The meat has a mildly gamey quality that can be improved or enjoyed as is.

Quail should be kept in low cages (not more than eight inches high, or the birds scalp themselves trying to fly), which can be purchased for about $30 for a trio of cages, or home-made for less. Generally, a 10"x10"x8" cage can house three or four birds. If a male is kept with two or three females, the eggs can be quickly incubated and hatched for new teeny babies which will be producing meat or eggs about two months after hatching. A pair of breeding quail may cost up to $15; day-old chicks may be less than $1 each. A few hatcheries sell fertile eggs.

The drawbacks of both chicken and quail are similar. Both produce a fragrant manure, which is pleasant to no one and must be aged (left to the elements) before use in the garden. If cages are moveable, or the chickens are "free-ranged" on a farm or small homestead, this build-up problem is less serious. Free-ranging chickens will result in some losses to predators. Roaming chickens will invade your garden, unless the garden is fenced.

Both quail and chickens are noisy, especially if male birds are included in your bunch. Roosters crow all day and occasionally in the night; they may try to attack children and small pets. Quail roosters make a nerve-wracking cackling sound. Your city neighbors will not enjoy either kind of rooster (although the occasional dozen fresh eggs might soften their feelings). Hens and quail will peck your hand when you try to retrieve eggs. While it's usually just a pinch, occasionally a bird will draw blood.

The sight of blood on another bird from a scratch or a pecking may send your other fowl into a pecking frenzy, resulting in the death or ghastly injury of the victim.

The birds need to be fed and watered daily, just like other livestock, and protected from predators. And butchering day is no more pleasant than it is when processing rabbits.

A few other types of stock are fairly easy to raise and care for on a small farmette or suburban acreage, such as a dairy goat ($100 more or less) and three or four head of sheep (around $50 per head). Both can provide meat (their offspring), milk (though the goat will give more and for a longer duration), and the sheep can supply fiber for spinning and knitting. Remember, too, that those adorable pot-bellied pigs are considered a menu staple in Asia — a pair of breeding-age adults runs less than $100 in my area, and can readily produce hundreds of pounds of offspring each year. These are not city animals, though, and will surely run you afoul of urban neighbors and the law. The time and energy commitment is much higher for these larger animals.

If you have not raised food animals before, please start with rabbits or chickens first. You'll save yourself a lot of grief. See the bibliography near the end of the book for more details on these animals.

BULK BUYING

If you're not inclined to grow your own foods, you can still stock up inexpensively by buying stuffs in quantity. Bear in mind that when you are buying already-prepared foods (such as TV dinners or microwavable burgers) you are also paying for the manufacturer's cost of putting the ingredients together. It is always cheaper to purchase the basic ingredients, and make your own meals from scratch. Clearly, bulk buying requires more ready cash than gardening, but it also takes less "food production" time.

In essence, you can acquire bulk foods in two ways: either by buying large single containers or by buying case lots. I buy my rice in 25-pound bags, and realize a fifty percent savings over the one-pound bag prices. Some markets also carry "institutional cans," holding three to five pounds of food such as tomatoes or creamed corn. These are less expensive, pound for pound, than smaller cans.

The size of a case varies from product to product. Most ordinary-size cans of vegetables, for instance, come packed in 12 or 24-item cases. A few products, such as cooking oils, may come six to a case. The quantity enclosed is always printed on the box.

The ideal time to buy in bulk is when your local store is offering sale items. Rather than buying one on-sale can of, say, tuna fish, you would buy the entire case. Most groceries (especially buying-club types or those advertised as "food barns") offer discounts on cases. The case discount, often ten percent, plus the sale price can amount to significant cost savings. (Watch for limits on sale items, such as "Limit 2 with an additional $10 purchase.") At the same time, it allows you to stock up a number of cans of one product quickly. It's very pleasant to stack a dozen cans of peaches, or bottles of catsup, onto your shelves.

The drawback of bulk-buying is that it is going to cost extra at shopping time. Instead of your ordinary food bill, you will have additional charges for each case included. If your budget is like mine, you won't be able to buy more than one or two cases of bulk goods each month. Of course, that's better than no storage.

MRE'S

There are many varieties of freeze-dried or dehydrated products in case lots, and as individual servings called Meals-Ready-to-Eat (MREs). These provide one or multiple servings of a cooked entrée, to which you must add water to reconstitute. If a person had nothing more palatable, these foods would be preferable to not eating; some are actually quite pleasant and flavorful. They are exceptionally easy to store and prepare, keep well for years, and are portable.

The first drawback of MREs is the cost. A sufficient quantity to last a family for a single month can set you back $1000-3000. They are unfamiliar foods, as I've noted before, so you should make a point of eating MREs at least once a week until they become familiar.

If you opt for MREs, please be aware that the military and the Federal Emergency Management Agency (FEMA) have the first priority in MRE sales — the companies that make MREs are often considered "emergency resources" by the Feds, and the government can demand the food use first as a "national security" priority. Therefore, you may have a several-month wait between the time you order supplies and when you can pick them up. It's better to order ahead of time than to wait until an emergency (such as Hurricane Andrew) arises and not be able to get what you want.

"BUDDY"-BUYING

A close relative of bulk buying is the buddy system. In effect, when you do your ordinary shopping, you simply buy one extra of each item — one is for you to use, one is for your "buddy," the pantry. Clearly, this works best with canned goods, or with things you will be able to preserve at home. And this is done most inexpensively, once again, with items that are on sale. The cost of the few extra cans hardly shows up on your weekly food tab, so it's not an ordeal, and can be managed on even the tightest budgets.

I buddy-buy my vital coffee supplies, getting two or three cans of the stuff whenever possible, and switching brands to obtain the best prices. My routine is to purchase sale goods up to the limit, and simply stick the extras in storage.

The main drawback to buddy-buying is that it is a slow way to accumulate goods. You may be able to store only a couple of extra items per shopping trip — better than not storing, but hardly a month's supply.

BARTER

My husband teaches the sport of fencing. He's traded lessons for many items: firewood, wool, and for grown pigs. Those two-hundred-pound hogs included transportation to the butcher shop, preparing, and wrapping to our specification. In effect, the 120 pounds of meat from a pig comes "free" — it costs us no money, only the time spent in teaching fencing.

Barter, which is covered in a later chapter in a different context, is an ancient pastime which predates the use of all currencies. The ability to barter is a *learned skill*, though... not something you can develop overnight. Bartering for foods, however, can be as simple as making an offer.

Once, a single gent had fruit trees laden with peaches, plums and citrus. He also had lots of quart canning jars, but neither the inclination nor time to put up the gallons of fruit. He asked me to can the fruit for him, in exchange for half of the results. How could I resist?

One year, we were raising two piglets. Two different people offered us excess milk from their goats and cows, in exchange for some of the pork. The hogs grew remarkably fast from the high quality milk, and the flavor of the meat was superb. Everybody was happy, including us... the pigs had cost much less to raise because of the additional milk!

The only barter rule for you to consider is "know the value" — of both your offering, and of what you are trading for. And be flexible. If you keep your eyes open, you'll find barter opportunities all around you.

The drawbacks of barter include the fact that you may not be able to find *exactly* what you want in a trading situation. Flexibility and adaptability are big pluses when working out a barter arrangement.

Furthermore, there is always the possibility of misunderstanding between parties to a barter, as well — so details should be worked out clearly and unambiguously.

FORAGING/HUNTING

It is the fantasy of some part-time survivalists that, come the collapse, they will be able to "live off the land" by hunting and foraging for foods. It's the rare individual who has actually tried to survive based on whatever they could find in the wilderness — especially during a severe crisis situation, when everyone else is trying to do the same thing.

Foraging and hunting for survival are not the same as doing so on a camping outing. The reason our ancestors turned to the reliable production of agriculture is because foraging provides such slim, unpredictable pickings. Not only that, hunting deer and other edible protein is often protected by conservation regulations; you can go to prison for taking a deer out of season these days.

Which isn't to downplay the value of both wild vegetables and meats. In our region, blackberries grow like weeds along roadsides and in old pastures — and they can be picked in summer by the gallon loads for jams and preserves. Wild acorns provide a significant addition to our routine diet, when the nuts are gathered in the fall. There are also abundant walnuts, hickories, raspberries, all kinds of wild greens, cattails and forgotten apple trees, as well as groundhogs, snapping turtles and squirrels for the taking — not to mention the many varieties of edible mushrooms.

But when considering foraging or hunting to increase the food-storage supply, you don't need to trek to the wilderness. You'd be surprised at the amounts of perfectly edible foods going to waste all around you, even in major cities.

For instance, spring and fall in Southern California are superb times to harvest olives. Some communities, such as

Thousand Oaks, have planted the trees as ornamentals —
and the well-tended plants drop thousands of pounds of
olives on manicured lawns all over the region. A diligent
forager, who wouldn't mind stocking up, could gather a
year's worth of olives for oil and for marinating in a day or
two.

All over the nation, people have fruit trees in their yards.
When we lived in a city, we watched orange and lemon trees
drop their fruit to rot on the ground — homeowners
apparently don't know what to do with the stuff! I've also
seen apricots, plums, figs, persimmons, peaches and guavas
left for the birds; the sheer waste is incredible. Yet, if you
offer the homeowners a quick yard "clean-up" by removing
the excess fruit from the trees, they are often pleased to be
rid of it.

Lawns with "unsightly" dandelions offer ingredients for
salads and cooked greens. Fallen pine cones contain "pine-
nuts," a gourmet item. Stately old street-lining maple and
birch trees can be tapped for their syrup in early spring.
County parks with flowering crab-apple trees provide the
makings for jams and jellies. Tall date palms drop edible
fresh dates along roadways. If you live in or near a city, take
some time to drive around and look for these free feasts —
the quantity of foodstuffs right on people's doorsteps is truly
astonishing.

It will be useful for you to acquire a guidebook to edible
wild plants for your region (see the bibliography). Don't eat
any strange plant without being absolutely certain that it is
safe. If you aren't sure, don't eat it. NEVER eat a mushroom
unless you're POSITIVELY SURE it's safe.

When we think of hunting, we often overlook edible
smaller animals. Doves, pigeons, blackbirds, starlings, frogs
and even snails; all provide excellent nutrition — and a few
are considered delicacies. City neighborhoods often harbor

opossum, squirrel and other tasty victuals. Just don't try to eat ones which are easy to catch or which appear ill.

A real drawback of foraging is that it is seasonal: you must know the ripening and harvest times for your foods. For instance, summer dandelions are too bitter to eat, while spring ones are tender and sweet. You also must collect the ripened goods all at once, then prepare or process them immediately to avoid spoilage. All of this requires lots of time, and that must be at the *right* time. Finally, you must be concerned about chemical sprays used on lawns and parks; they may make foods toxic.

Drawbacks of hunting are that you must actually be able to do it — it's not as easy as it looks. You'll need a weapon for dispatching your kill (most likely a rifle or shotgun), and the inclination to clean and process the carcass. You'll need lots of time to locate and stalk the game, too.

Lastly, if you wish to include foraging or hunting in your food-storage program, you should plan on keeping at it continuously. These are learned skills of the highest order.

GLEANING

A friend brought us a surprise one day: several large crates full of slightly-crushed pints of strawberries, about fifteen heads of wilted cabbage, and around fifty pounds of tired-looking sweet potatoes. I quickly canned everything and ended up with 10 pints of strawberry jam, 12 quarts of sauerkraut and 20 quarts of sweet potatoes — equal to about $54 worth of grocery-store purchases.

What my friend neglected to mention, until much later, was that he'd acquired the edibles from a dumpster behind a supermarket. It was all produce that had become "unsellable" due to damage or injury. It was a shock — but the food was perfectly useable, if a little on the rough side. Besides, it was free.

Gleaning, the gathering of unwanted foods, is another ancient art. It's mentioned in the Bible as one of the many ways to help poor folks acquire foods (see Ruth). Like foraging, it requires time and energy but has a very low cost.

Gleaning supermarket dumpsters may sound like the lowest of the low methods of food gathering — but I know a farmer who has made a science of it. He arranged with the produce manager of a small market to pick up the damaged veggies once or twice a week "to feed my rabbits." Once a month or so, he brings a freezer-fryer around to the manager. Both are pleased with the situation: the manager doesn't have to toss out the food, and the man gets "rabbit food" free. He does feed a little bit to his bunnies, but the majority of the food is prepared and stored by his wife.

Most fast-food restaurants have regulations about how long food may sit under heat lamps. At closing time, late in the evening, all cooked foods must be thrown out. Dumpsters behind these establishments — as well as at larger restaurants — often have pounds of cooked left-over fries, pizza and fish steaks in them. Used frying oils make excellent soaps, when strained; and can be added to pig feeds to quickly fatten them.

Countryside gleaning is a little bit more like recycling. Corn farmers harvest with large heavy machines, which don't collect all of the corn. When asked, these farmers often allow gleaners to clean up the fields of leftover ears. The last harvest days at "pick your own" operations have the smallest and least-pretty edibles left on the plants. Field managers allow both some gleaning and some half-price buying. Orchards may allow gleaning of windfall fruit.

As with everything else, there are *drawbacks to gleaning*. You won't be getting the best, freshest or finest-looking foods. Dumpsters are not clean places and are frequented or slept in by unsavory individuals (who haven't missed the opportunity to glean a little, as well). There is the possibility of exposure to disease if foods have set around for a while (never glean raw meats for this reason) — or if cooked foods have been mixed with leftovers from customers' plates.

It is also a very "downscale" method of acquiring food, even if it is done through legitimate channels. The emotional connotations of poverty and "trash picking" are often enough to keep people from trying this very accessible system... which is probably why dumpsters remain full of edibles.

PUTTING IT TOGETHER

The best total food acquisition system makes use of each one of the previous methods, as they become available. At present, we have sheep, dairy goats, chickens, ducks, geese, pigs and rabbits, which provide our meat, milk, cheese, ice cream, eggs, and fiber needs. We garden almost all the vegetables and fruits we use (except for citrus and bananas), and barter for apples. We forage for blackberries, raspberries, wild strawberries, elderberries, acorns, wild herbs, and take the occasional turtle for the table. As a consequence, my 1994 supermarket bill (which includes shampoo, paper goods, cocoa, sugar, bleach, coffee and other locally-ungrowables) was $38 per week. This included both the goods we consumed and those we put into storage.

Even so, we ate well — better than most, probably, given our "fancy" meats — and didn't worry at all about where the next meal was coming from.

If you think this is because we were raised in a conservative country household with a "use it up" philosophy, you're wrong. We're city-born and -educated, with a "spend, spend, spend at the mall" orientation. The transition from earn-and-spend to earn-and-save was hard-won... but if we could teach ourselves how to put up and store food economically, you certainly can, too.

FOUR:
HOW TO PRESERVE
AND STORE FOODS

When you store mass-produced canned goods, your main consideration in storage is how to stack and use the older cans first (more on this in the next chapter). If your food acquisitions are more varied than canned goods, you will have some decisions to make on food-preservation methods. The time-tested approaches are: freezing, pressure canning, water-bath canning, salting or brining, smoking, vinegar pickling, fermenting, root or cool cellaring, drying and brandying. As with the food-production methods, there are pro and con aspects of each preservation approach, as we'll see.

As with food production, storage can often best be accomplished by making use of many different methods. For instance, I pressure-can, smoke and jerk our meats, have frozen lots of stuff (when we had continuous electricity), have made jams, pickles, kraut, fermented milk into cheese, and kept potatoes in cool storage.

Clearly, the method you use will depend upon your available time, finances and taste preferences. I prefer frozen peas, but now pressure-can peas for lack of a freezer — freezing is easier, but if you don't have it, you must go for second best!

FREEZING

This is probably the most familiar and simplest method of preserving fruits, vegetables, cooked items and meat. Purchased frozen stuff, such as ice cream, can go directly from the supermarket into the home deep-freeze. And home-produced goods can be frozen for long-term storage with a minimum of supplemental work and supplies. Most vegetables simply need to be "blanched" (boiled for three minutes) and quickly cooled in cold water before packing into jars, plastic boxes or freezer bags. Meats can be frozen direct from the store, or as soon as the animal's body heat has dissipated, or after allowing freshly-butchered carcasses to age for several days. Most berries and small fruits can be frozen as-is, and larger fruits like peaches can be skinned and frozen in slices. Even eggs can be frozen, simply breaking them together, beating slightly to mix, and freezing in an ice-cube tray — when thawed, each egg-cube is the cooking equivalent of a beaten whole fresh egg. It's quite convenient.

An important consideration in keeping frozen goods is the "freezer life" of the product. Most fruits, vegetables and meats will keep in near-perfect condition in zero-degree-Fahrenheit temperatures for three months. After three months, foods begin to gradually lose quality — even when very well-wrapped. Fruits which are frozen in sugar syrup tend to keep better, due to the preservative powers of the sweetener. After about six months of solid freezing, vegetables will have become drier and will have a somewhat stringier texture than the fresher product. According to food authorities, most meats become relatively unpalatable after nine months of freezing. There will also be a certain amount of nutrient loss over time.

Even so, remember those stories of Arctic pioneers finding frozen woolly mammoths, those elephant-like creatures which died out at the last Ice Age. The explorers found that cooked mammoth steaks were quite tasty...and those had been frozen for around 10,000 years. I've found "forgotten" meat in the bottom of my freezer that had been there for, perhaps, four years. Except for "freezer burn" (drying) on any exposed parts, and sometimes a slight "freezer flavor," it's always been perfectly palatable. In an emergency situation, I'd certainly prefer to consume old frozen meat rather than go without.

The drawbacks of freezing include the cost of purchasing storage bags, jars, or plastic boxes; the cost of the freezer itself; and the continuous electricity needed to keep it running and cold. Used freezers that are fairly reliable can always be found in the $100-300 price range. The chest-type freezer is somewhat more efficient, since cold isn't lost as readily when the door is opened.

Probably the biggest difficulty with freezing is the concern that power might be lost for an extended period of time during an emergency situation. Short-term part-day outages generally don't hurt a full freezer because of the stored cold within the system, but if power will be off for days or possibly weeks, then foods will thaw and perish. During an emergency, the usual suggestion of adding dry ice to the freezer may become impractical or impossible. Therefore, if you have a significant portion of your foods frozen, it would be wise to include a back-up system — such as a small generator to power the freezer for a few hours each day, enough to keep things fairly frozen until they can be used or canned. (Keeping that generator in good condition and with fresh gas or diesel handy becomes another problem in itself.) Even so, a freezer excels in convenience.

PRESSURE-CANNING

If you wish to can vegetables and meats, they must be pressure-canned. (Fruits, jams, pickles and the like need only water-bath canning.) Pressure-canning is accomplished using Mason jars, lids, or metal cans, and a heavy-duty pot made expressly for high-pressure cooking and preserving. Most foods are slightly pre-cooked, then placed in Mason jars (no other jars, such as mayonnaise jars, can withstand the pressure), and the sealed canner is then heated to ten pounds of pressure at 240 degrees Fahrenheit. Most vegetables take a half hour at ten pounds pressure; most meats and meat combination dishes such as soup require ninety minutes at ten pounds pressure. Pressure-canning is the only way to absolutely insure long-term shelf storage of canned vegetables and meats.

With pressure-canning, there is very little change in the product as it sits on the shelf— it is about the same a year after canning as it was an hour after canning. The pressure process destroys enzymes, bacteria and most other undesirable organisms in food. It cooks the life out of the food, as well, so no further cooking beyond rewarming is necessary after opening your jars. (Some authorities recommend boiling canned meats and vegetables for twenty minutes before tasting, but I can't imagine what nutrition or flavor would be left after all that cooking.)

While it is generally recommended that pressure-canned foods be consumed within a year of processing, foods can remain quite useable two or three years after canning.

There will be some slight loss of nutrients over time, though most nutrient losses will have occurred during the processing itself.

Pressure-canned foods are best stored where it will get neither very hot nor very cold. Heat may cause the seals on the lids to soften and leak; cold may freeze and shatter the jars.

There are drawbacks of pressure canning, which include the cost of the canner ($90), canning jars or metal cans, lids and other related equipment such as jar-lifters. You also must have a continuous, steady heat source on your stove — either electric or gas. You really can't keep high, continuous, even heat under a pressure-canner with a wood cook-stove (I've tried). Once the pressure is building, the canner needs constant supervision, as well — under high pressure, they have been known to explode with deadly effect. The lovely filled glass Mason jars can fall from shelves and break, costing you all your work, the food, and the jar.

Time is a consideration when pressure-canning. The correct processing time is counted from the point where the canner reaches ten pounds of pressure and 240 degrees on a "pressure gauge" atop the canner. But it often can take an hour or more to prepare meats or vegetables, then pre-heat the product, place it in jars, seal the jars, and place them in the canner — then the canner itself must be sealed and allowed to build up heat and pressure, often taking an additional half-hour to forty-five minutes. After the processing time has been counted, there is an additional cool-off period before you can open the pressure-canner. My canner will hold only seven quarts or eighteen pints of product at one time, so a single "round" of canning can take three hours from start to finish. It takes days to can a single hog or quarter-side of beef, so the meat-in-waiting also needs to be kept cold.

Pressure-canned foods may develop a deadly toxin caused by botulism microbes. Generally this shows itself by an off-smell, strange bubbles in the food liquid, or swelling of the jar lid. This is a very real danger of canned foods, but not a common one by any means. Statistically, about ten people per year die of botulism, but there's no point in becoming a statistic yourself — if a canned good seems the least bit suspicious, dispose of it; or, as the saying goes, "when in doubt, throw it out." That twenty-minute boil may help kill botulism spores, but it doesn't change the effects of the botulism toxin which may be in the suspect food. Maintaining good processing technique and following directions scrupulously prevents problems.

WATER-BATH CANNING

In this process, hot foods in sealed jars are placed in boiling water for ten to fifty minutes. There is no need to heat to "pressure" levels as in pressure-canning — the boiling temperature of water at 212 degrees Fahrenheit both cooks the product and kills undesirable bacteria. Botulism spores simply don't survive in the sweet and acid environment present in fruit and pickles.

Fruits generally are placed in a boiling sugar-based syrup (two cups sugar to two cups water for a medium syrup), heated slightly, and then sealed in jars and canner-boiled for a half hour. Jam, the mashed or puréed fruit product which is sometimes thickened with pectin, is handled in a similar fashion. Pickles are often treated to a short water bath when they are prepared for storage in jars.

Boiling-water canning is only suitable for fruits (including tomatoes), pickled goods, and fruit products such as jams. The foods come out much like supermarket canned fruits but with better flavor and color. They can be eaten directly from the can without additional cooking unless you want it. (If you try to can meats or vegetables using long-term boiling instead of pressure, the kind of canning that was done by great-grandmother, you flirt with botulism.) If you've never canned before, water-bath canning is a good way to start.

When looking at *drawbacks of water-bath canning*, the cost of supplies is the primary shortcoming. You'll need a large pot for boiling which will allow water to cover your jars by two inches (a pressure-canner can do double duty here, with its petcock valve left open so no pressure is applied). You will need canning jars which may include Mason AND mayonnaise-type containers, lids, rings, jar lifters and pot-holders. Sweetener isn't vital, but produces a better-colored and -flavored product; honey can be used, though there will be a change in the flavor of your foods.

Fruits can go off when canned — they can acquire odd but harmless colors, strange but harmless white deposits in the bottom of jars, and may actually begin to unpleasantly ferment and cause the lids to pop. Most problems with water-bath canned fruits are the result of failure to follow directions, not heating the fruit sufficiently to prevent floating, or using mineral-rich water. Canned fruits that have gone off are pretty obviously bad and can make you fairly sick if you are silly enough to eat them — so don't.

Canned pickles can become soft or mushy, but more likely the pickling process itself led to spoilage (see the info following). "When in doubt, throw it out..."

SALTING AND BRINING

This process has been historically used with nearly every food product, but is best used with certain types of strong-flavored vegetables (cabbages, kale, turnips, etc.), sea fish, and "salt" pickles. Salt can be used to preserve some firm fruits such as blueberries, but most fruits do better under canning or freezing.

A brine is made by adding plain (not iodized) salt to water, the concentration depending on the product to be preserved. (Iodized salt will change the food's color.) A 10% solution, one pound salt to 9 pints of liquid, prevents the growth of most bacteria; a 20% solution of one pound salt to 4 pints liquid stops even salt-tolerant bacteria. Brining is used when the product — such as vegetables — doesn't release much of its own natural juices; otherwise, adding salt without extra liquid, or "dry salting," can be done.

Generally, with juicy or finely-cut vegetables, adding 2-½% salt by weight (that is, 2.5 pounds salt to 100 pounds of vegetables) will ferment or "sour" the product — like sauerkraut. Adding 25% salt by weight (2.5 pounds salt to 10 pounds vegetables) will simply preserve them without fermentation.

Meats can be salted, either prior to smoking as a part of the curing process or as a preservative in itself. "Corned" beef (or lamb, chevon, you name it) is a salted meat, prepared using a brine "strong enough to float a potato." The salt is dissolved in water until the hypothetical potato will float, and then the trimmed, cooled meat is added and covered with the brine. Left in a refrigerator for about three weeks, it will be fully "corned" and ready to lightly cook and eat. (I wouldn't use this with pork or bear because of the possibility of parasites in the meat.)

Salt, in fact, is so versatile as a simple, safe preservative that keeping fifty pounds on hand would be wise on general principles. Fresh animal hides can be salted to preserve them prior to tanning, and salt is indispensable in cooking. Unless you live on a sea coast, it's one of those necessities that simply can't be produced at home.

As to the drawbacks of salting and brining, they are both health- and storage-related. First, high quantities of salt in people's diets have been connected with high blood pressure and other health disorders. There are a sufficient number of other methods of storing food so that those suffering from these conditions shouldn't have to include salting as a preservative. Furthermore, meats that have been heavily salted often need to be boiled prior to use to flush salt from the tissues.

Salting foods requires large crock-sized containers or 5-gallon food-grade plastic buckets, a place to store these large items, and the willingness to keep checking on the preserved foods to be sure they are covered by the brine and that no unwanted insects or vermin have climbed into the containers.

Salted and brined foods can go bad, becoming mushy, slimy or generally rank-smelling (which isn't to be confused with a layer of goo that forms atop the brine and needs to be removed every so often). Foods that have gone bad simply haven't had enough salt added — this can happen when the food contains more liquid than expected in recipes, or when the proportions of salt to liquid are incorrectly measured. Try again with a thoroughly cleaned container and fresh foods.

SMOKING

After brining or "curing," nearly all meats can be smoked. Hot smoke, in which the temperature of the foods reaches 150 degrees or higher, is a method of smoke-cooking foods. Cool smoke, from 90 to about 120 degrees, is a system for adding smoke flavor to foods while drying and reducing possibilities for spoilage.

Hot smoke is used when you wish to "smoke-barbecue" food and you plan to consume it very soon or preserve it by freezing, drying or canning. It can be used, with care, for long-term storage if you don't mind very dry meats. Cool smoked meats can be kept in cool dry storage, or may be either frozen or canned for long-term keeping.

Although Grandpa used to cure and smoke meat for long-term keeping, he generally used that fall ham up by spring ("Easter Ham" was often the last of the pig), so that it never really was exposed to the heat of summer. Grandpa also had to boil his ham prior to baking to help get the salt-cure out of the tissues. Today, you can purchase "cures" which contain preservatives such as sodium nitrate and sodium nitrite. Both additives have a poor reputation among health-food people; however, using these cuts down on excess salts in the meats. It's a trade-off; several books in the bibliography have recipes for no-preservative cures, but you must follow directions precisely.

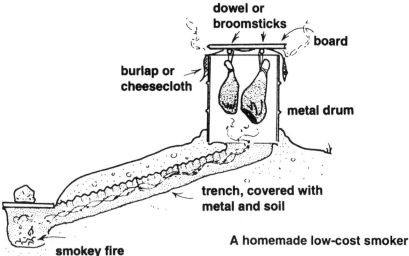

A homemade low-cost smoker

The drawbacks of smoking are the need for a smoker (you can purchases small ones, make them from metal drums, or go all-out for a concrete structure), access to hardwood chips for smoke production, and the willingness to keep feeding the fire and wait for days or weeks for your goodies to be ready. Meats can go bad during curing and smoking, becoming moldy, rancid, or slimy. But you can't beat the flavor.

VINEGAR PICKLING

Relishes, dill pickles, pickled eggs, sweet pickles, pickled pigs feet — they all are the result of submerging a food product in a 5% vinegar solution. Foods are prepared, either by cutting or cooking or brining, and then placed in a heated vinegar solution. Sometimes sweetener, spices or other flavorings are added to the vinegar. The vinegar itself may be white distilled, apple cider, or wine — as long as it is not homemade. If you do use homemade vinegar, you must determine the vinegar's acidity — less than 5% acidity will not preserve your foods adequately. Finally, vinegar-pickled foods are canned and placed in a boiling water-bath for ten to twenty minutes. This preserves them indefinitely.

Vinegar pickling, except in the case of brined cucumber pickles, can be done in an afternoon, with jars and jars put up in no time at all. Brined pickles, though, must soak for weeks in the salt solution before they meet the vinegar. If you follow recipe directions it's difficult to go wrong on vinegar pickles.

The drawbacks of vinegar pickling include the cost of jars, spices, canners and other utensils, as well as the cost of the vinegar used. Plain white distilled vinegar is the least expensive, but it is worthwhile to buy the better brands. Discount brands often have less mellow and more astringent flavors.

FERMENTATION

Fermenting is one of the oldest and most reliable methods for preserving some foods, including milk, fruits and vegetables. These items, when fermented, are known as cheese, wine and kraut. Fermentation is carried on by means of a bacterial culture, either one that is native to the foods or an introduced culture. Introduced cultures give a more uniform and predictable end product — when you decide to make yogurt you end up with yogurt rather than some other substance.

Milk fermentation into cheese is quite detailed and complex, although fresh raw milk will automatically sour and separate into the beginnings of cheese: curds and whey. There are literally hundreds of types of cheeses, including yogurt and cottage, and each can be produced using a little ingenuity and a special cheese culture. Cultures can be purchased from supply houses, or you can develop a culture by placing an ounce of grated supermarket cheese into warm sterilized milk and letting it set overnight. All cheeses will continue to age while in storage, some becoming dry and crumbly, others becoming runny or filled with bleu mold. A cheese with unwanted green or red mold can still be scraped free of the colonies, and the unmoldy portions eaten. It's difficult to cause a well-made cheese to become inedible.

Fermenting fruits (and vegetables) into wine can be done in one-gallon or larger containers with the addition of sugar, spices and wine or cooking yeast. Like cheese-making, wine producing is both art and science — follow recipes precisely until you're ready to experiment. All fruits can be preserved as wine, and most vegetables (including onions, peas and carrots) make interesting and highly drinkable wines. The character of the preserved food obviously changes when fermented in this way — it probably loses a significant percentage of vitamin C — but it gains a kick from the alcohol produced during fermentation. Most fruit and vegetable wines are useable shortly after fermentation is complete, but the flavors improve dramatically after a year in storage. These items will continue to age and change (improve) the longer they are stored.

Krauting vegetables is a fermentation carried on by lactic acid bacteria — cabbage krauts particularly simply and reliably, although most vegetables can be krauted. The product can be thin sliced or grated, then added to a specific amount of salt or light brine, then left to go about its work. Like all fermenting products, the veggies will bubble and expand and smell incredibly potent, then return to a calm steady state when finished. Krauted vegetables can be left submerged in their original container if kept in a very cool location; or they may be water-bath canned. If kept cool or canned, they won't continue to ferment. Raw krauted vegetables contain a high percentage of lactic acid bacteria, which is supposed to be excellent in human nutrition.

The drawbacks of fermenting include the cost of equipment — cheese-making supplies such as large pots, skimmers, cultures, heat source, cheesecloth, cheesepress (or equivalent); wine supplies like buckets, cultures, hydrometer (not vital but useful), bottles, corks; kraut supplies, including barrel or bucket, jars, lids, — and the time to learn the skills involved. Cheese and wine making both can become lifetime avocations, with much to learn and gain from either one. All fermenting is aromatic (some would say smelly). And there are religious and philosophical restrictions on the fermenting of fruits and vegetables into wines.

COOL CELLAR

Cellaring foods is another of those ancient methods of preservation for which we do not know the origin. All the world's cultures have developed methods of underground storage, or cool storage, of foods. Basically, the food is placed in a hole or pit in the ground, then covered thickly. One-season holes are covered with hay, leaves or a layer of dirt. Permanent holes in the West are known as basements or cellars, and are covered with several feet of concrete and dirt or the owner's house. Generally, this method is used for firm vegetables and sound fruit.

Basement or cellar storage is acceptable if adequate ventilation is allowed into the storage area, and if the area never freezes. (Freezing and subsequent thawing will cause the foods to spoil.) There are methods of converting an ordinary basement into a food storage area of this type, which includes shelves and boxes for the potatoes, carrots, heads of cabbage and so forth. Effectively, cold storage is the ancient equivalent of a giant refrigerator, without the electric bill.

The drawbacks of cold cellaring include the need to continually monitor the foods (that one bad apple can literally spoil the whole barrel); the need to properly prepare and seal the storage spot; the inevitable problem of vermin; and the cost or effort of including a cellar or pit on your property. It works best in winter, adequately in spring and fall, and poorly in summer. You must consume everything from one year to the next.

DRYING

Careful drying of fruits, vegetables, and meats is believed to be the single best method of preserving the nutrition of the food involved. Using a low setting on an oven (pilot light or 120 degrees), a sun-heated receptacle or a special electric food dryer, drying food is almost as easy as freezing it.

Most fruit products are merely cut into slices or halves, may be treated with ascorbic acid or lemon juice to retain color, and placed in the dryer. Vegetables are sliced, then may be blanched in boiling water and placed in the dryer. To dry or "jerk" meats, the lean sliced sections are first treated with a flavoring solution which is either homemade or purchased, then set in the dryer. Foods are dry when they bend but do not snap apart, which may take several hours or days. Most herbs and spices are dried as the preferred method of preservation.

Dried goods take up a fraction of the space of conventionally-canned foods. A single quart Mason jar can hold a bushel of dried, powdered tomatoes — a tablespoon added to water makes a thick, tomato-y paste. All dried foods, with the exception of jerky, should be reconstituted in water prior to use; dried fruits don't have to be reconstituted for snacks, but most cooking recipes calling for dried fruit suggest a soaking period before use. Never, never consume dried vegetables without reconstituting in water — the food will absorb liquid from one's digestive tract and may cause all manner of potentially serious internal problems.

The flavor of dried foods, although pleasant enough, is unfamiliar to most folks. When planning to dry a majority of your food storage, first try out dried goods and sample recipes to accustom your family to the flavors.

The drawbacks of food drying are the cost of drying equipment (special driers for larger quantities of food may run to several hundred dollars), the continuous use of a power source (which may be electric, cooking gas or propane), and the jars for storage — fewer than conventional canning requires. Flavor may be a factor, as well. Dried foods must be stored where moisture, including humidity in the air, cannot get at them. Remember, too, that with dried foods you must plan on storing lots of extra water for reconstituting, so your water storage costs for containers and space will be increased.

BRANDYING

This is a rather unfamiliar method of preserving foods, although it was used throughout the eighteenth and nineteenth centuries extensively. Fruits can be stored whole in high-alcohol liquid which can be brandy, bourbon, vodka, rum or grain alcohol. The liquor should be 80-proof or higher for long-term preservation. There is considerable change in the food thus preserved — it packs a knock-out punch in the form of absorbed alcohol. The alcohol dries and firms the food, replacing the natural juices within the food with a high-octane fluid.

Brandying and alcohol preserving have been used for the making of fruit and spice liqueurs, those sweet after-dinner drinks and cordials. The fruit to be liqueured is mashed and steeped for a month in sufficient alcohol to cover, then drained and the resulting liquid sweetened to taste.

Brandying will preserve the food indefinitely. To use, the product is fished out of the alcohol and prepared for the table; no cooking is required. Even milk may be preserved by mixing it half and half with brandy. Bacteria do not survive in high concentrations of alcohol — at one time, alcohol was used by scientists and physicians to preserve bodies and dead animals for later laboratory use. Bear in mind that you must use *drinking* alcohol and NOT rubbing alcohol; rubbing alcohol can kill. The liquor may be reused, although it loses potency each time.

The drawbacks of brandying include the difficulty of finding recipes and the need for personal experimentation; the very high (and going up) cost of the brandy or other alcohol; the need for many and varied containers; and the usual religious and philosophical restrictions on the use of alcoholic beverages.

SUMMING UP

There's more than one method for storage; experiment to find what you prefer. Some foods will be easier for you to store using one system instead of another, will cost less because you have certain items already, or may taste better to you and your family because of previous association. For instance, I have both canned and dried celery for use in winter soups and stews. They both taste about the same, but a quart jar only holds a single celery plant when canned... two dozen plants of the dried dehydrated celery will fit into a quart jar. Drying is significantly more space-efficient, and the flavor is indistinguishable from canning when used in soups.

To start with, use the method that you enjoy most (or dislike the least) — in that way, you'll be more inclined to begin and continue storing foods. After you are comfortable with your favorite method, branch out and try another way. You'll keep from becoming bored with routines, and you'll find quicker and more economical methods on your own.

FIVE:
WHERE DO I PUT IT?

Supermarket canned foods have strange combinations of numbers and letters stamped or printed on them — these codes are indications of the processing date and "use by" date for the food inside. It's fairly common for home canners and preservers to write the processing date on their goodies (that's how I knew that chicken I found deep in my freezer was several years frozen).

But it's the rare person who dates their purchased goods; we tend to rely on the "good until..." date somewhere on the package. Actually, the foods you buy may have already been in the supermarket for some time before you bring them home — or they may have come in on this morning's shipment. Without a key to the coding on packages, you can only trust your purchasing date as an indicator of the age of the food.

It's pretty tedious to write the date on cans of green beans brought home from the supermarket — but it is quite an revelation to discover how quickly or slowly you use those items. The hand-written date is the only way to know for sure, and knowing for sure is the foundation of a food-storage system. Commercially-canned foods should be used within a year of purchase, though they might be safe for several years. Do try date marking as soon as possible; it becomes a habit, and you'll wonder why everyone doesn't dateline their food. You may use a permanent marking pen, a grease pencil or even a crayon.

Supermarkets "rotate" their food items, moving to the front of shelves those goods which are older. Customers take the food off the front of the shelf, just as you do with your preserved foods at home. It's apparent that one of the better ways to keep track of the "age" of your preserved foods is to store the older items IN FRONT of or ON TOP of the fresher ones. As you can imagine, this becomes a job in itself. The illustration on page 59 shows one way to insure that the older cans are used first.

Other than this simple mechanical means, the only way to use older foods up first is to rotate by hand. This is not quite as complicated as it sounds, since not all your food will be preserved or purchased at the same time. If you are canning apples, for instance, they are not in season until months after cherries have come and gone — if you are looking for an older canned fruit to prepare, your cherries will automatically be older than your apples.

When you have stored, say, apples and gone through a year to the next apple season — and you still have stored apples — those older fruits can be set aside for "first" use. Place the older goods in front of the new ones, and you will automatically use them first.

Frozen foods require a different system if you wish to keep good track of what's inside your freezer (you probably don't want to find that four-year-frozen bird). A spring cleaning — removing all the items to a cold spot, defrosting the freezer and putting the older stuff back on top of the newer items — will give you a chance to look over what's there. You may wish to keep older goods to one side of the freezer, or in a rack, so you can maintain track of them and cook meals around them.

Some people keep a written record of their freezer's contents, and have it posted on the freezer door. Each time new items are added, the list is increased. When something is removed, it is checked off the list. In this way, they keep track of freezer contents without having to dig around in the cold.

Here's a sample freezer record, which can be drawn up on lined paper:

ITEM	HOW MANY?	NUMBER USED	NUMBER REMAINING
Pint Green Beans	6	卌	1
Pt Wax Beans	15	卌 ll	8
Quart Strawberries	4	l	3
Quart Tomatoes	35	卌 卌 lll	22
½ Gal Ice Cream	3	ll	1
Cans Coffee	12	ll	9
Pork Chops-4 per	5	lll	2
Lamb Chops-6 per	8	卌	3

and so on. Make a listing for each item as you put it into the freezer, then check it off as it gets used. The "how many remaining" number changes often enough that you may wish to write in pencil — it's erasable.

I tried keeping a similar list for home-canned foods. Although it was interesting to see how much stuff had been put up, I didn't find the list useful — just a glance at the pantry shelf told me what was there and what wasn't.

However, stored food is no longer kept only in the pantry; there are homes where food storage becomes a genuine logistics problem for lack of a large "keeping room." In those cases, use of a list of what's in which place would be virtually mandatory.

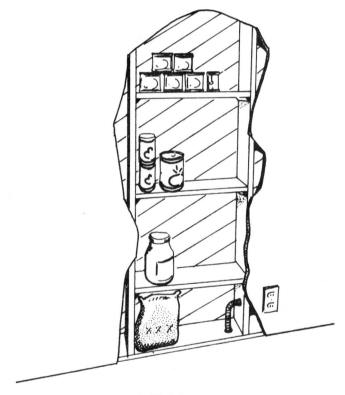

In-Wall Storage
The opening can be framed and finished for permanent use.

There is a surprising amount of space in even the smallest residences that can be used for storage. Under beds, in closets, stacked in boxes in corners as support for a plywood "desk top," in the back of cupboards which are securely attached to walls, behind books on wide bookshelves, under or behind the couch, inside shelves in a freeze-proof garage, and so forth. If jars or cans are placed inside of boxes, the boxes can be stacked and covered with an attractive tablecloth to provide a "coffee table" effect. Never store in the attics — the heat in summer will ruin jar seals, and it may be freezing cold in winter.

If you're really compulsive about food storage and haven't much room, the "empty space" between wall supports can be opened and fitted with shelves. The area is generally fairly narrow, about 3½" wide, but that's plenty for most cans and jars. To be extremely circumspect, the openings can even be recovered to appear as solid empty walls.

LARGE QUANTITIES, SAFELY- INEXPENSIVELY

One of the finest suppliers of nitrogen-packed grains offers thirty to forty pounds of whole wheat in highly portable white plastic five-gallon buckets. These storage specials run around $22 per bucket. In contrast, I've been able to put up similar wheat berries, in similar five-gallon food-grade buckets, for about $3 per container. How?

First — the buckets. You can purchase quality food-grade (suitable for holding foods because they are a particular type of "stable" plastic) buckets with lids for about $5 each. They're worth it, too, but these gems are being tossed out at supermarket deli departments, fast-food shops, and food manufacturing plants every day.

We spotted a stack of around 24 of these behind a fast-food restaurant in a small town — they were sitting beside a dumpster. We asked the restaurant manager if he'd mind if we took the buckets. He agreed, but said we'd have to take what was in them, as well. Every one was filled to the brim with used cooking oil. The manager considered this a useless waste product, and just wanted to be rid of it.

What a treasure trove! If purchased new, the value of the buckets (which had once held "crinkle-cut pickles") was $120. The used cooking oil, almost all of it, was eventually fed to our chickens and pigs — reducing the cost of feeding those animals, and increasing their productive output. Furthermore, a friend wanted to try making soap: she boiled and cleaned the oil from a single bucket and had a great, inexpensive time experimenting with recipes.

Never let a plastic five-gallon bucket get away from you — they are one of the most useful items you can find.

Second — the wheat berries. The CEO of a food chain created a media flap a few years ago by saying that poor people could find incredibly cheap food in this country — at the livestock feed store. He suggested that feed corn could be ground for corn meal and corn bread; milk-replacer powder for calves could be made up into drinkable whole table milk; and crushed oats for horses could be cooked into breakfast oatmeal. The media was horrified: animal food fed to children!?!

In fact, many animal feed grains are exactly the same as grains used for human food, with the exception of looks. Human grains — such as wheat, corn, barley and oats — are graded (in part) by how large individual kernels are, and how "clean" (free of weed seeds and foreign particles) it is. After harvest, grains destined for human or animal consumption are stored in the same structures, transported in the same trucks and barges, sprayed with the same fungus-inhibiting chemicals. Both are subject to the same atmospheric and vermin pressures (mold and mice). Neither animals nor humans should eat grains that have become moldy or bug-infested, so a lot of effort is made to prevent those problems.

The main difference between animal grains and human grains, naturally, is cost. Whole wheat berries, for animals, cost about $4 to $5 per fifty pounds in the Midwest. The same for human consumption is around $15 when bought in bulk — and up to $65 if bought in smaller packages. My preference, always, is to buy the least-expensive grains destined for human consumption — but I'd prefer to store animal grains rather than nothing at all. (Please be certain that we are talking of *whole grains* such as corn, wheat, oats and barley, here — not of pelletized animal feeds or grain mixes such as "super stocks." Don't ever use anything except whole grains... you simply don't know what is in the other stuff.)

In effect, whole feed grains can be safely consumed by people, with only a few precautions. I'd check with my feed grain dealer to find out what sorts of sprays have been used on the stored grains, for starters. (My local feed store explained that they sell grain so quickly that they don't need to spray for resident vermin or molds.) I'd also be exceptionally choosy about the quality of grain I stored, rejecting any that showed grey or black powdery coatings (molds); or any that were off-color, especially if the grain is pink — that's a fungicide the grains have been dipped into, and it can kill you. (Feed grains are never sprayed that pink color — that's for grains intended for planting, not consumption.)

HOW TO STORE IN PLASTIC BUCKETS

Grains, beans, pasta, flour, rice, sugar — all these and more stable foods can be readily "put up" in those wonderful five-gallon buckets. You need to keep a few basics in mind: protection from the plastic itself, sealing, and protection from insects.

Foods should not be stored in direct contact with the plastic bucket. While "food grade" buckets are extremely stable, there is a slight "leaching" effect that takes place between the plastic and the food stored in it — the food can pick up undesirable chemicals or flavors from the plastic, particularly if stored for years. I do not know of any cases of illness caused by this leaching effect, but protecting against it is so simple that it's worth doing anyway: Storage food should be put into brown paper sacks first, or left unopened in the supermarket bags it came in. That's it.

After packing the bucket as full as you can, place the lid on it and press down the rim solidly, all the way around the top — there should be a "click" as the lid fits down securely. To make certain that this is as bug- and air-tight as possible, tape the lid with several strips of duct tape. Cover all the little slots on the lid, and press the tape tightly against the plastic. Use a black indelible marker pen to describe the contents ("Mixed Pastas, 15#"), and record the date the bucket was packed.

Preventing insect damage to your bucket-packed foods — even home-grown grains — can be done very simply. After the bucket is packed and sealed, place it in your deep freeze. This is the method used by "organic" grain firms, who don't want to use chemical bug killers. Keep your bucket hard-frozen (zero degrees Fahrenheit or below) for at least four days; two weeks would be better. This freezing kills any living bugs which may have slipped into your goods, and it also destroys larvae and eggs of insects. The duct tape used for sealing buckets should keep new six-legged intruders out indefinitely.

The buckets stack readily, two or three buckets high, but they do take up quite a bit of space. Basement, garage or cold cellar are idea places for these buckets. Remember to rotate these containers, too.

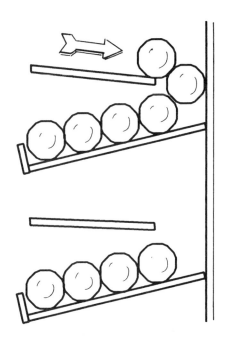

Gravity-fed storage shelf, in profile cross section.
Should only be used for goods in metal cans — not glass jars.

SIX:
BARTERING —
AND OTHER THOUGHTS

In the event of a severe disruption of deliveries to supermarkets, some food items will simply cease to exist in most parts of the country. For example, in the Midwest and most heavily-populated coastal areas, salt might become scarce. Since iodized salt is vital to maintain health (prevent goiters) in the middle sections of the country, there's a good chance it will become a "prime" valuable commodity. Wars were once fought over salt, remember, and the desire for spices such as cinnamon and cloves was what drove explorers around the world five centuries ago.

In those most difficult circumstances, a supply of hard-to-acquire foods might be more valuable than money — even more so than gold or silver. Both precious metals are useful in hard times, but where food is scarce even foolish people won't trade food for metal. Unless they have a surplus.

Barter foods are goods bought specifically to use for trade during severe calamities. During World War II, chocolate, nylon stockings and cigarettes were traded as a type of underground currency.

One survival-food enthusiast suggested storing only one-pound cans of coffee as a barter good — they're very stable and durable — and had apparently filled a closet in his apartment with the stuff. While I applaud his good taste and planning (and especially with my dire addiction to the stuff), I believe his emphasis on a single product was shortsighted. Suppose he can't find anyone willing to trade edibles for coffee?

If you want to know what goods will become valuable in the event oi severe disruptions, ask yourself this: *What foods will I want that I won't be able to produce myself?* The ones you want are the same ones other people will want.

Your list might include: coffee, cocoa, salt, sugar, pepper, soda mixes (small and easy to store), hard liquor, chewing gum, yeast, baking soda and assorted spices. How about other things like toilet paper? canning-jar lids? jars themselves? plastic wrap? condoms? ammunition? vitamins? perfume? quality soaps? canned cigarette tobacco and papers?

An extra supply of any one of these items may give you leeway to barter in an unstable economy. How much is a package of cocoa worth? A single pack here today costs about two dollars. If cocoa cannot be purchased through ordinary channels, that package will suddenly escalate in value — it may be worth a lamb, a few chickens, dozens of eggs, a bag of flour, tires for your car or any number of other commodities. Or it may be worth just a package of cocoa. If you store extras of any barter goods, they will always retain their original value — and could be worth much, much more in a disruption.

I'm not advocating price gouging here, either. No one *must* have cocoa, or coffee or hard liquor; these are desirable items, but not vital for existence. "Gouging" takes place when vital supplies, such as water, are priced high because of scarcity. By storing barterable goods, you're not preventing anyone else from doing the same, or robbing anyone of something they need to live. You are simply making a guess about objects you believe may increase in value. This is the essence of entrepreneurial investment capitalism.

When you wish to arrange a barter for one of these rare commodities, it would be wise to imply that you only have a single package available to you — and that with extreme difficulty, saying in effect, "I may be able to come up with a can of cocoa in exchange for that lamb, but I'm going to have to do some asking around first."

Let's not be overly paranoid about this, but during a crisis some people forget about civilized manners and laws. It's best not to announce that you've got a pile of very desirable goodies stuffed into your unprotected pantry.

In the same way, it's best for very young children not to know too much about what is stored or where, since they may innocently say the wrong thing at the wrong moment. Older children may or may not be trusted with this important "family secret," depending on their personalities.

In the event of a very severe disruption in the social fabric of this country, you'd be well advised to keep your food stores in two or three different secure places. If you are confronted with hungry marauders, you can direct them to "your food supply" in one of the storage areas — your other food spots will remain safe for later use.

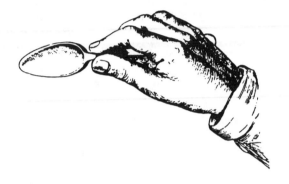

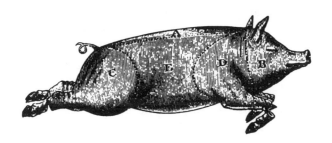

APPENDIX ONE:
BASIC HOW-TO'S OF
FOOD-PRESERVATION METHODS

This is a generalized description of food-preservation methods, and can be used as a guideline to saving foods when you have no other instructions on hand. However, it would be wise to consult more detailed and specific recipes, which can be found in books listed in the bibliography, if you plan to do extensive preservation.

Freezing: Almost everything can be successfully frozen for storage, although some foods will change texture or become mushy or crumbly when defrosted.

Freeze fruits as cut slices or mashed purées, covered with a sugar syrup (2 cups sweetener to 1 cup water). A few fruits, such as berries, can be frozen whole on trays and dumped into plastic baggies for storage.

Vegetables, except for tomatoes, should be cut to desired serving size, placed in boiling water for three minutes (corn on the cob blanched for seven minutes), then plunged into icy cold water. Drain and package. This blanching prevents further undesirable changes in the veggies, and helps retain color and flavor.

Meats, even supermarket ones, should be packed in freezer paper in serving-size packages. Use freezer tape to secure and label with type of meat, cut, number of servings or weight, and the date of freezing ("beef, chuck steak, five pieces, 3#, 6/1/95"). Home-processed meats must be thoroughly cooled before freezing (all body heat out of the meat). Chickens and other fowl benefit from being held in the refrigerator for up to three days prior to freezing — otherwise, they'll turn out tough as leather when cooked. Beef and deer should be "hung" for one to two weeks. Lamb, goat, domestic rabbit and hog can be hung, but can also be frozen when completely cool without detriment.

Tomatoes should be prepared as a sauce or purée before freezing — takes up less space. Frozen whole tomatoes will thaw into a pile of mush. Citrus fruits can be juiced for freezing, or frozen whole in their peelings — thaw completely in the refrigerator and then consume as juice. Bananas can be frozen whole in their skins. They defrost quickly and can be peeled before fully thawed; if thawed, they will be very leaky and mushy. Frozen bananas can also be partially thawed until peelable, then eaten like a banana popsicle.

In case of freezer failure or power outage: a fully loaded freezer at zero degrees will keep foods frozen for two days or so, depending on the weather. A half-filled freezer can't be expected to stay cold for more than a day.

Fifty pounds of dry ice, placed atop boards or blankets over the food (never directly on the food) will keep the whole thing solid for around two to four days. NEVER TOUCH

DRY ICE WITH YOUR HANDS — use cardboard or extra heavy gloves to handle the ice.

Lacking dry ice, cover the freezer with blankets or insulating material, and don't open it. If the freezer will be off for an extended time, start canning or drying the contents, eating frozen goods before you use food saved by other methods.

Pressure-Canning: Use clean Mason jars only, making certain in advance that there are no nicks or cracks in the rim.

Carefully check your pressure-canner, inspecting petcock, safety valve and rims. Have the pressure gauge tested annually at Extension offices or by sending to the manufacturer according to their directions. If the canner or lid has ever been dropped, do not use it — hairline cracks may not be visible, and when under pressure can cause them to explode with deadly effect.

Meats and poultry should be cut into chunks, removing excess fat, bruises and gristle. Fish should be soaked in salt water, drained and prepared for jars no larger than pints — half pints are better. There are many specific recipes, but in general, meats can be "raw" packed directly into jars. (Jars should be hot and clean.) Leave a full inch of space at the top, and do not force the meat in — allow it to settle on its own. Add a teaspoon of salt per quart; a half teaspoon per pint. Wipe rims clean to assure seal. Seal jars with lids and place in warm water in canner, which fulfills the manufacturer's requirements (generally two inches of water). Only make up enough cans to do a single canner load at a time.

Heat canner with lid on and petcock valve open. When steam escapes freely for two or three minutes, close the petcock valve and begin closely watching the pressure gauge. Pressure will slowly build up — allow it to reach 240° F, 10 pounds pressure, then gently adjust the heat to maintain this temperature. Begin counting the canning time from full pressure. Meats are kept under this temperature and pressure for 90 minutes, more or less (check specific recipes). Do not leave canner unattended! When time is up, turn off heat and let the canner cool without moving it. When the pressure has reached zero, open the petcock valve — there should be NO burst of steam. Carefully unlock and remove the canner lid, tilting it away from you as you do so. The jars will still be very hot, their contents bubbling vigorously. If any jars have cracked, the contents will be mixed with the water — throw jars, contents and water away.

Let the jars cool where they are for about fifteen minutes. Remove jars from the canner to a draft-free counter and let them finish cooling for several hours. Remove lid bands — lids should remain tightly sealed to the jars. Test seals by gently pulling upward on lids — if any lids come off, you can either recan the stuff, starting from step one, in a clean jar with a new lid; or you can briefly store the food in the refrigerator and consume it in the next day or so.

Vegetables should be canned using the same process, but canning time is seldom over an hour. Many vegetables require only a half hour of pressure — you must refer to charts for specifics.

Canning Time Tables (in Minutes)
At 10 Pound Pressure Unless Otherwise Indicated

Product	Pints	Quarts
Beef Chunks	75	90
Hamburger	75	90
Fried Brains	80	90
Bologna	75	90
Hash	75	90
Boiled Tongue	75	90
Fried Liver	45	50
Kidneys	70	80
Heart	75	90
Pork Chunks	75	90

Product	Pints	Quarts
Pork Sausage	75	90
Spare Ribs (Bone Out)	75	90
Chicken Pieces	65	75
Roast Fowl	70	80
Wild Duck	85	95
Rabbit	75	90
Squirrel	75	90
Fish Chunks	90	---
Crab	90	--- (5 Lbs Pressure)
Oysters	50	---
Clams	90	---
Lobster	90	---
Shrimp, liquid	90	---
Frog Legs	90	---
Milk, Very Fresh	20	25
Pork & Beans	85	105 (15 Lbs Pressure)
Meat Soup Stock	20	25
Asparagus	25	30
Lima Beans	40	50
Beans (the seeds)	65	75
String Beans	20	25
Beets	30	35
Carrots, Turnips	25	30
Broccoli, Cauliflower	25	30
Cream Corn	95	---
Whole Kernel Corn	55	85
Eggplant	50	60
Hominy	60	70
Mushrooms	30	---
Okra	25	40
Green Peas	40	40
Black-eyed Peas	35	40
Sweet Potatoes	65	95
White Potatoes	35	40
Pumpkin	65	80
Spinach, Other Greens	70	90
Chard	55	60
Squash	65	80
Veg Soup Mix	40	45

Water-Bath Canning: This process is used to can high-acid foods such as pickles, fruits, jams and tomatoes.

Fruits should be peeled, pitted and cut into slices or serving-sized chunks. They can be treated to prevent darkening with ascorbic or citric acid, or by soaking for a few minutes in a solution of 2 tablespoons each of vinegar and salt to a gallon of water. Jams are made from crushed fruits and sweetener, which has been cooked until it thickens. Fruits can be canned in a sugar syrup ("medium" is 3 cups sugar to 4 cups water). Boil the syrup, heat the fruit until heated through, then place fruit in sterile hot jars, cover with syrup, wipe rims clean, seal. Place in very hot water in the canner and fill with hot water until the jars are covered by at least two inches of water. Bring to a boil and begin timing. Boil for the full time period recommended.

Turn off the heat. Use "jar lifters" to pull the heated jars from the canner and set on towels or wooden boards (jars may crack if set on cold surfaces). After jars have cooled, remove bands and test lids for seals. Label, date and store.

Foods to be pickled, except cucumbers, are briefly boiled, then heated in a vinegar solution which may contain spices or sweetener. Pickles are given a short water bath, perhaps 15 minutes; the vinegar is a powerful preservative.

Tomatoes are actually a fruit which is used like a vegetable. They are fairly high in acid, but some varieties lack that important substance — a tablespoon of vinegar should be added to each quart of canned tomatoes to be certain there is sufficient acidity. A teaspoon of salt per quart can also be added. Tomatoes can be canned whole, crushed, sliced or even boiled down to a thick paste-like texture. Don't add other ingredients, unless you plan to pressure-can the product.

Product	Canning Times for Water Bath Pints	Quarts
Apples	15	20
Apricots	20	25
Berries	10	15 (not strawberries)
Cherries	10	15
Figs	15	20
Juices	10	10
Grapes	15	20
Gooseberries	20	25

Product	Pints	Quarts
Peaches	20	25
Pears	20	25
Pineapples	30	30
Plums and Prunes	20	25
Strawberries, crushed	15	15
Tomatoes	50	55
Tomato Juice	20	20

Salting. Dry salting for storage is different than curing meats — for the items that follow, add one cup salt per four cups vegetable. These cure best in those old-fashioned heavy crocks, but you can use glass gallon jars just as easily. Food-grade plastic will work, but I'd be somewhat concerned about the leaching effect if the food was stored for long periods.

Corn, greenbeans, greens, peppers, turnips, etc.: Steam or boil the vegetable for ten minutes. Cut corn from cobs, grate or cube turnips. Mix food with salt, four cups food with one cup salt. Pack into crocks or containers. Cover well with cheesecloth or muslin and hold down with a clean weighted plate. Brine should form within 24 hours and be visible and cover all the vegetables. If insufficient brine, mix 3 tablespoons salt with 1 cup cold water, and pour over — continue until brine covers vegetables. Replace cloth and plate.

Store in a cool place (below 40 degrees F), but not frozen. This will cure and be finished in three to five weeks. Scrape off any foamy muck which forms on the top.

When you wish to use, dip out sufficient amount for a single meal using a clean glass or plastic scooper — never metal, since it may color or contaminate the brine. Soak the vegetable in several changes of clean cold water. When the veggies taste freshened (most salt out of it), cook gently in a little water. Serve as usual.

Smoking. Hot smoking, 150 degrees or hotter, is used to prepare foods for immediate consumption (or for canning or freezing) rather than for long-term storage.

Cold smoking, keeping the food in 70- to 120-degree smoke, is used for preparing for storage. The food, most often meat, is dried and flavored in the process. Afterwards, it should be stored in a cool, dry place — or it can be frozen.

Examine the diagram on page 42 for a homemade smoker. The fire should be ten to twelve feet away from the smoker so that the smoke cools sufficiently. Slant the smoke draft up from the fire at about 30 degrees (this angle is not depicted exactly in the illustration).

Meats may be cured using supermarket mixes. Hang foods so that they do not touch each other or the sides of the smoker. Start the fire, using damp corncobs or hardwoods only (apple, cherry, maple, oak, etc.); softwoods and pines leave undesirable flavors in the food. The food may be cured in eight to ten hours, or may need several days — you'll have to keep checking to be sure. (Cut a small slice out of the product and prepare as you ordinarily would.) Meats should be dry-looking through to the bone, with perhaps an outer layer of greasy residue (which may be wiped off).

Foods will smoke most uniformly if the fires are kept going day and night so that the smoking time is uninterrupted. If the fire goes out at night, this is all right if evenings are cooler than forty degrees F. If nights are warmer or the climate is very humid, the meats should be refrigerated during the evening until the fire is started the next morning.

Making quality smoked foods is truly an art — your first tries will certainly result in tasty foods, but the smoke may not have penetrated sufficiently to provide good long term storage. Remember that grandpa's smoked meats were stored in the smokehouse through the winter, and that by spring they were completely consumed. Even well-smoked foods should be kept refrigerated, frozen, or in a cold room protected from vermin.

Vinegar Pickles. Pickles and relishes can be made from any firm vegetable or fruit. Cucumbers are most often used for conventional pickles. The jars should be put through a boiling water bath to assure long term storage. Use fresh, just-picked ingredients for best results. There are two types of pickles: long brine and quick. A recipe for each type follows:

QUICK DILL PICKLES: Makes 3 quarts or 6 pints.

```
4    pounds sliced, cubed, or chopped cucumbers
3    cups vinegar (white or cider)
3    cups water
3    tablespoons canning (not table) salt
1    tablespoon mixed pickling spices
3    tablespoons dill seed
20   whole black peppers
(Optional for kosher-style: 2 garlic cloves per jar)
```

Sterilize jars by dipping in hot water. Pack with cucumbers and distribute spices evenly among jars. Combine vinegar, water and salt, and bring this to a boil. Fill jars with boiling solution to ½ inch from the top for quarts, ¼ inch for pints. Wipe rims clean. Seal. Put in boiling water bath, 20 minutes for quarts, 10 minutes for pints. Remove from water. Cool. Test seals. Label and store. Flavor develops in 6 weeks.

QUICK SWEET PICKLES: This is a "bread and butter" type.

```
4    pounds unpeeled sliced ¼-inch thick cucumbers
2½   cups cider vinegar
2¾   cups sugar
1¼   cup water
1    teaspoon celery seeds
1½   teaspoon pickling salt
1½   tablespoons whole mixed pickling spices
(Optional: ½ tsp. turmeric if yellow shade is desired.)
```

Combine sugar, vinegar, water and spices and bring to a boil to dissolve sugar. Add cucumber slices and bring to boil. Simmer for two minutes. Put into sterile canning jars while boiling hot. Wipe rims. Seal. These do not need water-bath canning — but if you wish, you can place in a water bath for five minutes to assure a solid seal. Cool. Test lid seals. Label and store. Full flavor develops after six weeks.

LONG BRINE PICKLES: Cut cucumbers into chunks.

4	quarts of chunked cucumbers
1½	cups pickling salt
16	cups water
4	cups cider vinegar
2	cups sugar
5	cups cider vinegar
3	cups water
2	tablespoons mixed pickling spices
1	tablespoon crushed cinnamon sticks.
3	cups sugar

Put cucumber chunks in crock or other suitable container. Dissolve salt in 16 cups water. Pour over cucumbers. Cover with weight to keep cucumbers under brine. Cover and let stand for 36 hours in a cool place.

Drain. Pour 4 cups vinegar over cucumbers. Add sufficient water to cover. Simmer 10 minutes. Drain. Discard liquid.

Combine 2 cups sugar, 5 cups vinegar and 3 cups water with spices. Simmer 10 minutes. Pour over cucumbers. Cover and let stand 24 hours. Drain, saving the syrup. Add 3 cups sugar to syrup and heat to boiling. Pour over cucumbers. Cover and let stand 24 hours.

Pack pickles into sterile jars, leaving ¼-inch space. Heat syrup to boiling and pour over pickles. Wipe rims. Seal lids. Place in boiling water bath for 15 minutes.

Cool. Check seals. Label and store.

Fermentation: One of the oldest methods of keeping fruits, milks and some vegetables — as wine, cheese and sauered "kraut." Fermentation is actually the process of decay, which has been carefully controlled and manipulated by encouraging specific bacteria and discouraging others. The end result is both nutritious and delicious — and the lactic acid bacteria which permeates many fermented foods is particularly good in human nutrition.

Wine and cheese are covered in separate sections in this book. "Sauering" is pretty straightforward and is quite similar to brining. Here's a recipe for cabbage, which becomes "sauerkraut" when finished. You can make up a quart or fifty pounds: Use cabbage, canning or table salt (not iodized), sugar, boiling water, (optional: ¼ tsp. caraway or dill seeds per quart jar, sliced onion, peeled garlic cloves, more or less to taste). Clean and sterilize jars and lids. Grate cabbage or cut into shreds as thick as a dime. Pack firmly into heated jars, sprinkling with spices if desired. Leave one inch headroom. Add 1 tsp. salt and 1 tsp. sugar (or ½ tsp. honey) to each jar. Fill slowly with boiling water and let settle. Leave ½ inch headroom. Wipe rim and seal. Invert gently, and set upright.

Place all the jars together in a cardboard box or other container and put in a cool space, around 70 degrees. This space should be someplace where you won't mind the smell of the kraut forming. The lids will bulge over the course of the next two to three weeks. If juice comes out around the lids, simply tighten the bands a little. After six weeks or so, the kraut is done. Wash the jars and store in a cool place — it will keep for at least six months. If you want long-term storage, place the jars in a canner filled with cool water and heat to boiling. Boil for twenty minutes. Cool. Test seals. Label and store.

Drying (Dehydration): One of the easiest methods of preserving foods. All vegetables should be "blanched" in boiling water or in steam for three to seven minutes (longer time for corn on the cob and thick vegetables) — the idea being to inactivate enzymes to prevent changes in the food after it is dried. Cut, slice or chop into uniform pieces. Remove corn from cobs. Peppers, herbs, onions and garlic don't need blanching. Fruits should be halved or sliced, then treated with citric-acid or vitamin C-based products to prevent darkening (available at the supermarket). You may also soak fruits for ten minutes in a gallon of cold water with a tablespoon of salt and of vinegar added to prevent darkening — results are not as uniformly light-colored as the supermarket product will make them.

Place in direct sunlight, covered by cheesecloth, and keep hot (about 130 degrees) until dry. Or place in gas oven with the pilot light on or at lowest setting (150 degrees). If you have a dryer, follow manufacturer's instructions. Leave foods until they are leathery to crisp, eight to fifteen hours.

Drying takes a certain amount of hands-on practice to get the most desirable results. When you wish to use the food, you can rehydrate by soaking in boiling water for a half hour or so — or just add dried vegetables to soup stocks, etc.; they'll rehydrate as they add flavor.

Brandying: When done the traditional way, brandying is the process of completely submerging foods in 80-proof (or higher) grain alcohol and storing it in hardwood casks. All foods prepared this way will keep indefinitely; the alcohol dries and firms the product and protects it from spoilage. The food also absorbs some of the alcohol. It becomes strongly flavored and fully capable of intoxicating the consumer.

Brandy is the favored preservative for this method, but any strong alcohol will do. NEVER use rubbing or wood — methyl — alcohol; it will kill you. All distilled alcohols are expensive — if you distill your own, have it tested for alcohol percentages before use to be sure it is potent enough. The alcohol will flavor the food, so you should enjoy the taste of the alcohol you use.

Since there is a dearth of hardwood casks around, you could use glass or stainless-steel containers — food-grade plastic will certainly leach after a period of time. Make sure the food is completely submerged, weighting it down with a Mason jar filled with water, if necessary. Cover securely.

Modern recipes call for the use of brandy as a flavoring agent, not as a preservative. For brandied peaches, for instance, you would rub whole peaches to "defuzz" them, and fill a quart jar without squashing them. Then add one cup sugar to one cup water and heat to boiling. Pour this, plus 2 tablespoons of brandy, over the peaches, leaving ½ inch of headroom. Wipe rim clean. Seal and process in a boiling water bath for 20 minutes. Cool. Test seals. Label and store.

Liqueurs and cordials are made by soaking mashed fruits or spices in pure distilled alcohols, such as vodka or brandy. There are many, many excellent recipes (see the Bibliography) — here are two examples:

Strawberry Liqueur — 3 cups fresh mashed strawberries, added to 3 cups vodka. Soak for two weeks. Strain, saving vodka mix. (The mashed fruit can also be used, if you wish, as a topping.) Filter vodka mix through cheesecloth and set aside. Mix 1 cup white sugar with ½ cup water, bring to boil. Cool. Add sugar syrup to the vodka/fruit mix. Let blend for one to two weeks. Ready for use.

Coffee Liqueur — Add two cups water to two cups sugar. Boil until sugar is dissolved. Add ½ cup instant-coffee powder or crystals. Add 2 teaspoons vanilla extract. Let this cool to room temperature. Now add 1½ cups good quality vodka or dark rum. Cover tightly and shake. Let rest for three weeks. Ready for use. Makes about a quart.

APPENDIX TWO: RECIPES FOR HOMEMADE GOODIES

MAKING MOZZARELLA CHEESE, INEXPENSIVELY

All hard cheeses known on this planet are produced using the same process: warm the milk, curdle it, separate the results into curds and whey, work the curds and dry the new cheese. The step in which milk is curdled also calls for a cheese culture and rennet, which are explained in more detail shortly.

While you can spend a small fortune to set up an at-home cheese factory, you can also inexpensively duplicate those expensive cultures and devices with a little thought and effort. The equipment necessary for cheesemaking can be found in nearly every kitchen.

A FEW WORDS ON RENNET

Rennet is a substance historically derived from calves' stomachs, and is used solely to curdle the milk. Milk *will* curdle on its own, provided it is left to sour naturally, but the results are unpredictable (though still edible). Rennet can be purchased in tablet form, which is made from the stomachs of slaughtered ruminants, and in a liquid form made from a vegetable or mushroom base. The vegetable rennet adds a slight bitterness to the finished cheese, which often isn't noticeable. Both tablets and liquid cost $3.00 to $6.00 for a quantity sufficient for about thirty pounds of cheese.

For hard-core self-sufficient types who prefer not to spend *any* of their cash, milk can also be curdled with infusions from certain wild-harvested or garden-grown plants: Lady's Bedstraw, nettles and thistle flowers. Harvest the herb; dry out of the sun. Make a strong "tea" from the plant material, using one handful of herb to one cup of boiling water; let cool before using. The amount you'll need will vary by the quality of your herbs — keep a record of the amount you use so that you can adapt your recipe to reflect the changes. Herbs may alter the taste of your finished cheese, too.

A slaughtered calf, lamb or goat kid, can also supply rennet. The animal's fourth "true" stomach should be removed and cleaned, then thoroughly salted and hung to dry. When crackling dry, it can be stored in a cool dust-free place. At cheesemaking time, a piece of the stomach approximately the size of a quarter should be cut off and soaked in cool water for about three hours. This liquid is then used in place of the rennet solution.

"STEALING" CHEESE CULTURES

Homemade cheese can be "stolen" from commercial cultures, in much the same way that yogurt can be started from a supermarket carton of the stuff. Here's how: Find a variety of Mozzarella cheese that has a flavor and texture you really enjoy. Make sure it has a good "stringy" quality, or select a "string" cheese (which are actually Mozzarella types). This should be a true cheese, not a "pasteurized process cheese food product," which contains no living cultures.

Grate off about three tablespoons of cheese. Take a quart of raw or pasteurized milk and place the liquid in a capped Mason-type jar, heat to near-boiling; allow to cool to a warm-to-the-touch 115°F. Open the jar and toss in the three tablespoons of grated cheese and recap. Shake vigorously. Put the jar in a yogurt-maker or warm spot (wrap in a wool blanket, or set the jar in 115-degree water inside another pan, or put the jar in a gas oven with just the pilot light on — you get the idea). In four hours to overnight, this milk will "set up" into a thick, yogurty culture. It'll have a layer of cheese at the bottom, remnants of the grated stuff you added.

You'll only need a cup or so of this culture to make up to three pounds of Mozzarella. The rest can be poured into a suitable freezer container and hard-frozen for later use — or you can consume it just like yogurt. It'll keep in the refrigerator or a cold spot nearly unchanged for about a week; if left at room temperature it will become more and more tart, eventually separating into curds and whey!

MAKING MOZZARELLA, DAY ONE

This cheese is so good that you should make as much as possible per batch — otherwise it all gets consumed at the first meal. Making two pounds (or five pounds, for that matter) is as easy as making one pound. This recipe is for three pounds of finished cheese; it can be adjusted to your quantity of milk. One gallon of milk makes about a pound of cheese.

Ingredients:

3 gallons whole milk (cow's or goat's or a combination is acceptable).
1 to 1½ cup culture starter
¼ rennet tablet or liquid rennet made according to package directions, or homemade version
salt to taste — "canning" salt, if you have it

Equipment: containers to hold and keep milk warm; a clean, scrubbed thermometer (dairy, candy, or outdoor are fine); long knife or spatula; real cheesecloth or clean muslin sheets cut to size; very hot water; very cold water; two wooden spoons or rice paddles.

1. **Be conscious of strict cleanliness. Run boiling water through or on all equipment (except thermometer) and allow them to cool before using!**
2. Warm milk to lukewarm, around 90 degrees. Add the "stolen" culture and the prepared rennet, stirring for at least two minutes to mix thoroughly. Cover the milk and set so that it can be kept warm and still for an hour (wrapping in a blanket is acceptable).
3. After an hour, uncover the milk. It should now be a thick solid curd, possibly with a pale liquid separated off. (If it isn't solidified, your culture is pooped-out or the milk contained some antibiotic residues that prevented the culture from setting it up. You can add more culture and try step #2 again, or start with fresh milk from another source). Take your long knife or narrow spatula and cut the curds — first in a north-south direction; then east-west; then from top to bottom. The idea is to make the curds into ½ inch square chunks. As you cut the curds, they will release liquid. This is the whey — suitable for human, pet or livestock consumption! After cutting, let the curds sit until they have settled to the bottom of the pot, about ten minutes.
4. Place a square of boiled and cooled cheesecloth or sheeting in a strainer over another container. Pour the whey through the cheesecloth into the container, keeping the curds in the cheesecloth. Let the curds continue to drip for a while, until they have firmed somewhat. Save the whey for other uses. Fold the cheese into the cloth, put the mass into a bowl and refrigerate overnight.

Day Two

The cheese curd needs a full day of resting so that it can develop the acidity which lends Mozzarella its delightful stretchiness.

5. Unwrap the curds and place on a clean plate or cutting board. Chop the firmed mass into ½ inch square cubes again. They may still drain a little whey; that's all right. If you like a salted cheese, you can sprinkle *lightly* with a canning salt, about a tablespoonful. Move the curds around with your clean hands; notice that they feel a little springy. You may taste them now, if you wish. The texture will change after the next steps are completed.

6. Heat a shallow pan of water to about 170 degrees — don't boil! Drop in a couple of cubes of curd. Use your two wooden spoons to press the cubes together. Notice what happens as you work these cubes — they begin to melt slightly, lose their shape, and cling together. Take the mass from the hot water and plunge into very cold water. It will firm up instantly... Mozzarella! (If the cubes don't want to stick together, let your remaining cheese curds rest for another hour or so — they're not quite acid enough.)

7. Now, take a good double handful of curds, and put into the hot water. Use your wooden spoons to work this as you did in the previous step, smashing the cubes together into a solid, clingy, rubbery ball. When you can lift the mass out of the water and it stretches away from you, plunge it into your cold water container. You've just made a pile of Mozzarella cheese!

8. Keep repeating step #7 until all the cubes are formed into cheese. You can experiment with shapes at this point, too — forming some into balls, some into those long "strings," some into pretzel shapes.

IT'S CHEESE!

When you take those shapes from the cold water, your Mozzarella is ready to use — make a pizza!

It can also be wrapped in plastic and stored in the refrigerator for a couple of weeks. Mozzarella freezes well for long-term storage.

I once left a ball of Mozzarella out to dry. I rubbed it with salt and turned it every couple of days. It developed a hard rind (I kept scraping off the blue mold which wanted to form on it), and matured into a rather bland hard cheese. We used this as a grated cheese in place of Parmesan over pasta.

As a final thought you can use the last three tablespoons of your homemade Mozzarella to start another quart of culture. Keep your cheese going in this fashion, and you'll never be without.

HOW TO KEEP EGGS

Your home-grown eggs can rest comfortably in the refrigerator or cold room for a month to six weeks without losing too much quality.

Freezing

Whole eggs: Wash the egg in cool water until free of dirt. Crack eggs, one at a time, into a small bowl and inspect for bits of shell or other unwanted materials and remove. Pour the egg into a larger bowl. Continue in this fashion until all your eggs are opened.

Carefully mix yolks and whites using a fork. Avoid beating air into this — it will leave you with tough end-results.

At this point, some people add either salt or sugar (corn syrup or honey may be used) to the egg mixture. Salt is added at ¼ teaspoon per three eggs, and is used when you plan to use the eggs for main dishes or omelets. Sweetening, added at ¾ teaspoon per three eggs, is included when the eggs will be saved for baking. The addition of either salt or sugar helps to keep the frozen eggs free of lumps — but I've frozen eggs without either additive. I never seem to know in advance how I'll use the eggs later.

Next, pour the egg mix into ice cube trays, or place three tablespoons of egg per muffin cup into oiled muffin pans. Freeze until rock hard. Empty the frozen "individual eggs" into plastic bags or put inside freezer containers. Label and put into the deep freeze. When you want to use a single egg for cooking, just pull out one of these egg cubes and thaw until soft. Then treat it just like a fresh egg.

You can also freeze a number of eggs mixed together for using in special dishes. Be sure to label with quantity of eggs in the mix, and what the planned use will be.

Egg yolks: Separate white from yolks. Mix the yolks very lightly. If you wish, add 1½ teaspoon sugar or ½ teaspoon salt to each half-cup of yolks. Freeze in single tablespoon quantities, representing one egg yolk — or in larger quantities to fit your recipes. Label carefully!

Egg whites: Separate whites from yolks. Don't mix or beat these at all. Freeze individually at 2 tablespoons per ice-cube tray section, or as a combined quantity. Thawed whites can be as stiffly beaten as fresh egg whites.

Frozen eggs keep for nine to twelve months.

Water-Glassing

This is one of those old methods of egg preserving that Granny probably used when faced with an egg excess. Old crocks often show the tell-tale white film around their interiors which is characteristic of water glassing.

Water glass is actually sodium silicate, a sealing compound which is still in use — though hard to find. Our local plumbing supply shop has been unable to come up with a supplier for two years, and gets many calls for the stuff anyway. If you can locate water glass, it's relatively inexpensive and quite efficient at sealing the holes in egg shells for long term preservation. It will also seal your plumbing shut, so don't pour excess into plumbing.

Use a large jar, canning jars or crock. Food grade 5-gallon buckets may also work, though I've never tried them. Pour boiling water into your container and clean thoroughly.

You will be using 3 cups of water to each ⅓-cup sodium silicate. Using an approximation suitable for your containers, boil and cool a sufficient quantity of water — this provides a fairly sanitized liquid to be used for storage.

Fill your container about half full with the cooled water, measuring as you go. Then, stir in the appropriate amount of sodium silicate.

Next, using a long spoon (avoid too much hand contact with the water glass), lower eggs into the solution one at a time. When your container is filled, leave about two inches of water glass above your eggs. Cover and date. Store in a cool place.

That's it! Water-glassed eggs will gradually become watery and lose their high yolks and firm whites — but can be stored safely at room temperature for four months, and up to a year if refrigerated or kept in a cool environment.

To use water-glassed eggs, pull out an egg with a slotted spoon and rinse in cold water (rinsing your hands as well, if you've handled the solution). Crack the egg into a cup or small bowl. If it looks and smells acceptable (no sulfurous odor), it's safe to use.

Should an egg break in your water glass, don't try to use it. The remaining eggs will still be safe, although the solution will become progressively more smelly. Other eggs may absorb the odor, so it's best to remove them from the solution. Store those eggs in the refrigerator or a cold place and use as soon as possible.

Pickling

Pickled eggs are a rather expensive delicacy these days (check your supermarket and prepare for a shock), but they are exceptionally easy to make at home. They can be stored at room temperature, and make delightful additions to salads, on canapé trays, for deviled eggs, sliced on ham sandwiches — and as a straight snack. What more could we ask for in a stored egg?

Use eggs which are at least a week old, though ten days to two weeks is better; otherwise they won't shell easily. Boil the eggs until hard-boiled (a good ten minutes at hard boil), then quickly dunk the eggs in cold water. Shell.

Sterilize quart canning jars by rinsing in boiling water, or pour boiling water into your preferred container. Place shelled eggs into hot jars (a quart jar holds up to a baker's dozen). For each quart, add a teaspoon salt.

Prepare a pickling solution, using your favorite unsweetened recipe or this one:

Mix three and a half cups any type of 5% (or stronger) vinegar to each half cup of water. Add a quarter cup or so of thickly sliced onions. Bring to a boil. Remove onions.

Pour this basic solution over the eggs. If you are using canning jars, dunk your lids into boiling water, put onto jars and seal. Invert the jars to slosh vinegar solution on lids. Then, let the jars cool. If using another kind of container, be sure eggs are completely covered by solution. Cool. Date and label.

If your vinegar solution was boiling hot and your eggs were still heated after shelling, the canning jars will seal. If your jars fail to seal, it's not a major worry — the pickling solution is strong enough to protect the eggs for some time. Keep unsealed jars in a cool place or in the refrigerator, and use first. I've kept pickled eggs for well over a year.

KEEPING "FRESH" MILK INDEFINITELY

There are three methods which result in acceptable drinking milk, though stored milk is a little different from the fresh stuff — but it's not an unpleasant difference, by any means. The methods are *freezing, condensing,* and *pressure-canning.*

FREEZING MILK

This is not the same as ice cream, and is not meant to be used frozen. It is probably the simplest method of keeping milk for an indefinite period of time, and the end result is virtually identical to fresh milk. You can use formerly-frozen milk as a "fresh" drink, or make custards, cheese, yogurt and so forth from it. The only drawback to freezing milk is that it takes up considerable freezer space.

Milk that is to be frozen should be as recently taken from the dairy animals as possible. Strain and filter, as usual. Pasteurize, if you are accustomed to doing that — though raw milk freezes just as well. Cool the milk as usual. Select very clean canning jars or plastic freezer containers.

If you have goat or sheep milk, simply pour into freezer containers, filling only three-fourths of the container to prevent bursting. Pop them into the deep freeze and you're done.

Cow's milk, however, will do best if you skim the cream first. Goat's and sheep's milk are "naturally homogenized" with their smaller fat particles, but whole cow's milk will separate as it's freezing and thawing and result in a jar of revolting lumpy goo which is good for nothing but doggie food. Freeze cow's cream and skimmed milk in separate containers, filling each only three-quarters full. If you prefer to drink whole milk, you can mix it back together after cream and skim have thawed.

Frozen milk should be thawed overnight in the refrigerator before use, and stored just as you would fresh milk.

CONDENSING MILK

Home-condensed milk is one of those projects that is most economical and enjoyable if it is done on a wood cookstove. The resulting product is similar to regular supermarket condensed milks and can be used in any recipe calling for condensed (not evaporated) milk. One real benefit of condensing milk is that is takes less space to store a quart's worth of condensed milk than whole milk — and the stuff can sit unchanging on the pantry shelf for a year. The significant quantity of sugar used in condensing acts as a preservative and flavoring for the product, which is both a benefit and drawback! Condensed milk can be used like fresh by diluting the final product with an equal amount of water, or used as is for a rich cream-like flavor.

Fill a large canner or stock pot with several inches of warm water. Using clean quart jars, place two cups of sugar and around two cups of milk in each jar and stir to blend. Cover jar tops with a piece of clean muslin or cheesecloth and screw on the ring band. Place the jars on a rack in the canner or stock pot and add warm water to the level of milk in the jars.

Set the pot on the back of your wood stove, or use a very low heat setting on your electric or gas stove. Heat to just below boiling, about 190 F degrees, and let this simmer. The temperature needn't be precise — it's just a means of keeping the pot warm enough to drive off moisture. Add hot water to the stock pot if the level dips significantly below the milk level.

The bad news is that it will take about two full days and nights of heat to reduce the milk by half. Each quart jar will yield about two cups of condensed milk. It can be used right away, or refrigerated for a couple of weeks. I have never tried freezing condensed milk, but it should freeze without much change in texture.

For long-term storage, prepare pint or smaller jars (according to your intended use) by washing and placing in boiling water. Keep your large canning pot nearby with the water still steaming.

Pour hot condensed milk quickly (use stove mitts) from quart jars into smaller jars to one-half inch from the top, clean rims, apply lids. Return the filled jars to the hot water, and bring the water to a boil. Boil for five minutes — just enough to secure the canning lids. Remove the jars from the canner and let cool out of drafts. Check for seal, label and store. If any jars have not sealed, store in refrigerator and use first.

CANNING MILK

The combination of high heat and pressure alters the milk and develops a cooked flavor in the end-product. It's just like fresh milk in texture, but nothing like fresh in flavor — it's better! Perhaps the closest flavor approximation is caramel candy, or the European cheeses known as Gjetost or Mysost. Canned milk can be used for cornstarch puddings, in coffee, or where you'd use fresh milk, but simply will not set up as cheese or yogurt.

Prepare canning jars and lids by washing and boiling. Get your pressure canner set up according to manufacturer's directions, having one to two inches of very warm water over the rack in the bottom. Bring milk directly from the barn and filter as usual. No need to pasteurize, since canning will do the job for you. While milk is still warm, pour into hot canning jars to one-half inch from top. The milk must be warm to start with (even if you must reheat it), or the jars will burst under pressure. The milk also must be super-fresh — or you'll end up with canned curdled chunky milk. Clean jar rims, apply lids and seal.

Place jars in the canner so that no jars touch. Close and clamp canner according to manufacturer's directions. Allow steam to escape vigorously for several minutes before closing vent. Heat canner to 240 degrees, ten pounds pressure, and hold quarts and pints at that level for twenty-five full minutes (counting from after the temperature and pressure are reached). If the pressure drops below ten pounds, you must start over and retime for the full twenty-five minutes.

Turn off heat and don't move canner until the pressure has dropped to zero. Carefully open steam vent. Do not try to rush the cooling process. When you can handle the lid screws, undo the canner top and remove with great care. Let the canned milk rest for fifteen minutes or so before removing from canner (the jars may still be bubbling internally for a while). Set the jars aside to cool completely. Check for lid seals, label and store each jar.

A use for pressure-canned milk is a variation on plain vanilla cornstarch pudding — it's a caramel delight which makes a light and nutritious mid-winter treat. Mix ⅓ cup sugar, ¼ cup cornstarch and ⅛ teaspoon of salt in a saucepan. Stir in 2¾ cups of cold canned milk and gradually bring to a boil over medium heat, stirring the whole time to prevent burning. The pudding will thicken considerably. Boil for a minute, then remove from heat and add two tablespoons of butter, margarine or oil. Cool or chill. The recipe can be readily doubled or tripled — and it's especially nice with a dab of whipped cream or swirl of chocolate syrup on top.

UNCOMMON WINES
(ANOTHER WAY TO SAVE THE HARVEST)

That homemade uncommon wines are easy to prepare is seldom obvious. The transformation of garden excess into a bright, sparkling, complex liquor is simpler (to my mind) than canning or drying a batch of anything. It calls for only basic, readily home-rigged equipment, the addition of commonly-available sugar or honey, yeast (even the cooking variety will do in a pinch), and perhaps a couple of lemons or oranges or a pound of raisins. The only truly difficult thing about making these unusual drinks is waiting for them to mature to full flavor.

ABOUT THE YEAST
AND THE AIR-LOCKS

Grape wine connoisseurs shudder at the thought of using any yeast but one made specifically for wines — and there are a dazzling array available for home use. Unless you have specific wine variety preferences, a Montrachet yeast makes a good all-purpose beverage. Many health-food stores now carry this kind of yeast. Nevertheless, a perfectly acceptable vegetable or fruit wine can be made with ordinary cooking (bread) yeast from the supermarket.

Air-locks can also be found at beer and wine-making shops, or you can construct an air-lock container fairly simply. The idea is to exclude outside air from the fermenting wine liquid, while allowing the beverage to expel excess carbon dioxide and other fermentation gasses. Some home-vintners have used a glass gallon juice jar, fitted a cork tightly in the top, and punched a narrow hole through the cork from top to bottom. Through the cork, a two-foot section of aquarium tubing is carefully inserted so that a couple of inches extend below the cork bottom, and the top edge of the cork is then sealed with wax around the tubing. After the jar is filled, the cork-and-tubing is fitted firmly in place, and the long end of tubing is submerged in a jar filled with water. As the wine ferments, gasses will escape through the tubing, and bubble up through the water — but no air will be able to enter the jar.

I've had good results using plastic gallon vinegar jugs, punching a hole through the plastic screw-on cap with a leather punch, and inserting aquarium air-line tubing. It fits so snugly that wax isn't needed. As a plus, the cap is easy to attach and remove from the jug.

THE PROCESS

Wine-making from flowers, herbs, fruits and vegetables is not complicated. Like all fermentation-based foods — such as cheese or bread — it requires an adherence to strict cleanliness and attention to detail. In each of the recipes that follow, the steps are the same:

1. Wash the vegetable thoroughly. "Garden Dirt" wine is not appetizing. Chop or cook and mash as directed.
2. Add vegetable to water; put in dissolved sugar and other chopped ingredients, except yeast.
3. Cool or warm the water and added vegetable to room temperature, or a shade warmer. Add dissolved yeast, and mix thoroughly. Cover container with lid or clean towel.
4. Set in room-temperature spot for about two days.
5. Strain off liquid into air-lock container. You can still consume the remaining vegetable "soup"; chickens and pigs can also get a share. Close and set up air-lock in room-temperature location.
6. Let continue fermenting for one to two months — until all bubbling ceases.
7. Transfer to clean holding container by siphoning (use aquarium tubing, or special winemaker's tubing). Leave sediments at bottom of air-lock as much as possible. Taste the wine while siphoning — it will be quite strong, possibly terribly-flavored or astringent. Don't despair! Once the wine has matured, the flavor will be completely different.
8. Add clean eggshells (washed before cracking), with some white still clinging, to the liquid. This will draw all remaining sediments to the eggshells, so that the wine naturally clears over several hours or days. Cover tightly with cotton wool or several layers of cheesecloth.

9. When wine has cleared, siphon into final storage bottles and cork, leaving behind shells and sediment. You'll notice that the flavor has already changed a little. It will continue to improve. You can use clean wine bottles or any type of sealable glass container. I've had good results with quart canning jars. Label with date of bottling, type of wine and winemaker.

10. Store in a dark, cool closet; under kitchen counter; or back of refrigerator. Don't bother to try the tomato or pea pod wines for at least a year — they are remarkably nasty until they've aged. Begin sampling the other wines after two months until they reach a flavor you like. Enjoy with a good meal!

RECIPES

Use the ingredients and follow the procedure previously outlined. Recipes are for a single gallon of wine — you can increase or decrease recipes to fit your container.

Carrot Wine
(Sweet, potent, and a dark orange shade.)

1   gallon and 2 cups water
5-7 pounds fresh carrots, cooked and mashed
4   pounds white sugar or 1 quart honey
2   whole sliced oranges
1   lemon (yellow rind and juice only)
½   pound raisins, chopped
1   package yeast

Onion Wine
(Delightful, pale golden and very intense — but no oniony taste).

1   gallon water
½   pound peeled, sliced onions
1   potato, washed and sliced thinly
2   pounds sugar
1   pound raisins, chopped
1   package yeast

Pea Pod Wine
(Can use empty pods, full pods or just shelled peas alone!
Makes a bright, white, earthy beverage.)

1   gallon water
3   pounds of pea pods, boiled until soft in some of the water
3   pounds of sugar or 1 quart of honey
1½ cups lemon juice
1   package yeast

Tomato Wine
(Let the mashed tomatoes rest in the liquid during the entire period
of fermentation, about 21 days. Stir every second day. Results in a
blushing golden wine, with a complex, distinctive flavor — no hint of
tomatoes!)

1   gallon water, poured boiling over tomatoes
10 pounds of chopped, mashed tomatoes
4   pounds of sugar
3   slices fresh gingerroot or ¼ tsp. powdered ginger
1   tablespoon salt
1   package yeast

Zucchini Or Other Squash Wine
1   gallon water, poured boiling over the squash
3-4 pounds peeled, diced squash
1,   cup lemon juice
3   pounds sugar or 1 quart honey
1   package yeast

Fruit Wine
But don't stop with these vegetables — use the same type of recipe with
any kind of fruit following these directions generally:

4   pounds crushed fruit, more or less
2   pounds sweetener
spices (ginger, lemon juice or dash citric acid, raisins) as desired
1   package yeast
1   gallon water

FAST AND FLAVORFUL JUICES

One of the speediest methods of "putting up" fruit of all kinds is to convert it to juice. Heat a gallon or more of water and make accessible for pouring. Sterilize jars (Mason and mayonnaise-type) by dipping or soaking in boiling water. Put lids in very hot water until ready to use.

Place hot jars on wood or towel; cold surfaces will cause jars to crack when filled. Put into each jar 1½ cup chopped, peeled (if necessary) fruit or berries, and ½ to ¾ cup sugar or sweetener. Fill jar with almost-boiling water to within ½ inch of rim. Put on lids and seal. You may gently shake these to mix the fruit and sugar — but do so very carefully... jars can crack or spurt liquid around the lid if moved when they are this hot. Let cool. Remove rim bands, check for seals. If any do not seal, you can reheat contents and try again. Label and store.

These are ready to use — that is, very full-flavored — in about four to six weeks. The juices obviously will contain pulp or chunks, so the liquid can be strained away, or the whole container put into a blender for a thicker drink. These are surprisingly good, with lively fruit flavor. Try mixing fruits for a "punch" drink.

"FRESH" FROM THE GARDEN
ON NEW YEAR'S DAY

It's January 1st. Outside, the wind howls and snow blows across an icy windowpane. Inside, you've just finished a holiday meal that included fresh homegrown melon and garden tomatoes.

An impossible dream? Not if you planted a little-known heirloom variety of watermelon or muskmelon, or a newer tomato variety, in last summer's garden.

Winter King and Queen Watermelon, Valencia Muskmelon and **Longkeeper Tomato** are three varieties noted for their long-keeping qualities. Picked just at the peak of ripeness, or slightly before, they will keep for months if stored at moderate temperatures (55-60 degrees) and turned occasionally.

Winter King and Queen (also called simply "King and Queen") is a round pale green watermelon, averaging 8 to 10 pounds at maturity — small enough to store readily. The flesh is a crispy pinkish red, very sweet and crunchy. When stored for long periods, the flesh becomes a little softer, but still retains that super-sweet quality. With each vine producing two or three fruit in 90 to 100 days, it needs the same cultural treatment as ordinary watermelon: plenty of compost buried under hills or in rows; 6 to 8 seeds per hill thinned to the three hardiest vines. Pick when the tiny tendril nearest the fruit has dried or shriveled for peak ripeness — or pick a little earlier. (Opinion is still undecided as to which harvesting method gives a longer storage time.)

Valencias (also called Spanish or Rocket Melons) are an unusual melon which originated in Spain. They are dark green, with a thick, wrinkled skin — and shaped something like a six-inch by eight-inch football. The flesh is a pale greenish-white, with a salmon orange tinge to the seed cavity. It, too, is very sweet — even after four or five months in storage. Cultivation is similar to watermelon or other cantaloupes: compost under hills, mulching the soil to retain moisture. Pick this melon after about 100-110 days when it has developed a yellow spot on its bottom side for maximum ripeness... it won't slip from the stem like other cantaloupe varieties. Again, you may prefer to harvest when underripe.

Both of these plants are open-pollinated so if you intend to save seeds (and why not?), don't plant within 100 feet of other varieties of watermelons or cantaloupes. They won't cross with each other, though.

Longkeeper Tomatoes are rather unique among the varieties of this favorite garden vegetable. Although they require the same basic cultural conditions as other types — a rich soil, caging or trellising the determinate plants, water during dry spells — they never achieve an intensely red color. They can be picked after reaching full size (3"-4"), and changing to a pale whitish-green. Some growers wrap each tomato in newspaper; others simply leave them in a cupboard or on a sheltered countertop. They will continue to ripen slowly for up to three months — and they're ready when they've turned to a pleasant sunny orange shade. The interior is actually a shade darker than the outside. While the flavor doesn't match a vine-ripened tomato, it sure beats the rock-hard supermarket ones available at the same time!

Sources for Winter King and Queen Watermelon include: Nichols Garden Nursery, 1190 N. Pacific Hwy, Albany, Oregon 97321-4598; and Redwood City Seed Company, P.O. Box 361, Redwood City, CA 94064.

Valencias can be found in few places except the Seed Saver's Exchange Catalog, Rural Route 3, Box 239, Decorah, Iowa 52101. Write for catalog prices and membership information. Gurney's catalog, and Henry Fields, both carry other types of long-keeping muskmelons, including "Emperor" and a hybrid "Rocket" type.

Longkeeper Tomatoes are listed in the Seed Saver's Exchange; and at Henry Fields Seed and Nursery Co., 415 N. Burnett, Shenandoah, Iowa 51602.

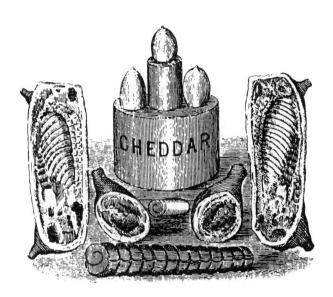

BIBLIOGRAPHY

FOOD PRODUCTION

How to Live on Almost Nothing and Have Plenty: A Practical Introduction to Small-Scale Sufficient Country Living, by Janet Chadwick. Published by Alfred A. Knopf, New York, 1979. A superb introduction to food gardening and small livestock production and processing.

Practical Skills, A Revival of Forgotten Crafts, Techniques and Traditions, by Gene Logsdon. Published by Rodale Press, Emmaus, PA, 1985. Chapters on food production, including gardening and livestock. If there is a better book on general subjects related to self-sufficiency, I've never seen it.

The Encyclopedia of Organic Gardening by staff of *Organic Gardening* magazine. Published by Rodale Press, Emmaus, PA, 1978. Resource that describes "all you wanted to know" about this method of gardening.

FOOD RECIPES AND TECHNIQUES

The Bread Book, A Natural Whole-Grain Seed-to-Loaf Approach to Real Bread, by Thom Leonard. Published by East-West Health Books, 17 Station St., Brookline, MA 02146 (paper, $8.95), 1990. Recipes galore — but also the unique and vital info on growing bread grains, and excellent instructions on how to make an outdoor bread oven.

Homemade Liqueurs, by Dona and Mel Meilach. Published by Contemporary Books, Inc., Chicago, 1979. Many recipes for making liqueurs from fruits, nuts and spices using store-bought alcohols.

Cheesemaking Made Easy, by Ricki and Robert Carroll. Published by Storey Communications, Pownal, VT, 1982. Sixty very clear recipes for different cheeses. A classic.

PRESERVING AND STORING

Managing Your Personal Food Supply, edited by Ray Wolf. Published by Rodale Press, Emmaus, PA, 1977. Very good general information with heavy emphasis on organic production.

Stocking Up, How to Preserve the Foods You Grow Naturally, edited by Carol Hupping Stoner. Published by Rodale Press, Emmaus, PA, 1977. This classic is updated periodically.

Putting Food By, by Ruth Hertzberg, Beatrice Vaughan, and Janet Greene. Published by The Stephen Greene Press, Brattleboro, VT 05301, 1974. This is perhaps the most comprehensive and useful preserving book on the planet. Updated from time to time.

Ball Blue Books, published by Ball Corporation, Muncie, IN. This series is updated every couple of years and is prepared by the company that makes the Mason jars — excellent recipes and very clear instructions. Available in major national department stores. A must-have.

FORAGING

Wild Edible Plants of Western North America, by Donald R. Kirk. Published by Naturegraph Publishers Inc., Happy Camp, CA 96036, 1975. Many color photos and quality descriptions; applicable in other regions as well.

A Field Guide to Edible Wild Plants, Eastern / Central North America by Lee Allen Peterson. Published by Houghton Mifflin Co., Boston, 1977.

GENERAL SELF-SUFFICIENCY

Back Home Magazine, PO Box 370, Mountain Home, NC 28758. Heavy organic/ecological orientation.

Backwoods Home Magazine, 1257 Siskiyou Blvd, #213, Ashland, OR 97520. Practical, conservative, down-to-earth.

The Mother Earth News — old issues number 1 through about 80. This is the premiere self-help magazine, but the current issues are just about useless. Look for old issues at garage sales and libraries.

Small Farmer's Journal, PO Box 1627, Sisters, OR 97402. Aimed toward people who use draft horses on small farms, but contains much useful and encouraging info.

Countryside & Small Stock Journal, W11564 Hwy 64, Withee, WI 54498. Reader-written, practical advice.

SEED STOCK SOURCES

Ridgway Hatcheries, Box 306, LaRue 7, OH 43332. Sends day-old chickens, ducks, goslings, pheasants, guineas, turkeys. Free catalog.

Murray McMurray Hatchery, Inc., Webster City, IA 50595-0458. Day-old chicks, ducks, goslings, pheasant, guineas, turkeys, partridges, and fertile eggs. Free catalog.

J. W. Jung Seed Co., Randolph, WI 53956. Family-owned.

Burgess Seed & Plant Co., 905 Four Seasons Rd, Bloomington, IL 61701. Low-cost.

Miller Nurseries, 5060 W. Lake Rd., Canandaiguia, NY 14424. Mostly trees and plants, extra cold-hardy.

Park Seed Co., Cokesbury Rd., Greenwood, SC 29647-0001.

Gurneys Seed & Nursery Co., 110 Capital St., Yankton, SD 57079.

Nichols Garden Nursery, 1190 N. Pacific Hwy., Albany, OR 97321-4580. Small family business.

Henry Fields Seed & Nursery Co., 415 N. Burnett, Shenandoah, IA 51602

R. H. Shumway's, PO Box 1, Granitville, SC 29829. Open-pollinated seeds.

Johnny's Selected Seeds, Foss Hill Rd., Albin, ME 04910-9731. Upscale, organic orientation.

Shepherd's Garden Seeds, 30 Irene St., Torrington, CT 06790. Unusual and European varieties.

The Redwood City Seed Company, PO Box 361, Redwood City, CA 94064. Family-owned, descriptive catalog. Some oddities.

Native Seeds/Search, 2509 N. Campbel Ave., #325, Tucson, AZ 85719. Plants specifically adapted to the Southwest, many unusual varieties.

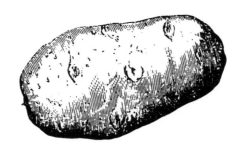

LAST WORDS

"It is useless for sheep to pass resolutions in favor of vegetarianism while wolves remain of a different opinion."
— William Ralph Inge, DD

"My people are destroyed from lack of knowledge."
— Hosea 4:6

"A very important point to realize in the case of a general breakdown is that men will become worse than beasts when they do not have food for their bellies, and they will be ready to pounce upon their neighbor, tearing him apart for just a piece of bread. We have seen... how even our own relatives

*and apparent friends betrayed us when it came to a
showdown."*
— Hans Schneider

*"If you do not believe that a man will commit murder for
one can of tomatoes, then you have never been hungry."*
— Robert A. Heinlein

*"The prudent see danger and take refuge, but the simple
keep going and suffer for it."*
— Proverbs 27:12

*"Do not let yourself be seduced into a false sense of
serenity by men who do not understand that the old world is
dead."*
— Robert A. Heinlein

INDEX

Other titles by Anita Evangelista:

☐ **14187 HOW TO LIVE WITHOUT ELECTRICITY — AND LIKE IT,** *by Anita Evangelista.* There's no need to remain dependent on commercial electrical systems for your home's comforts and security. This book describes many alternative methods that can help one become more self-reliant and free from the utility companies. Learn how to light, heat and cool your home, obtain and store water, cook and refrigerate food, and fulfill many other household needs without paying the power company! *1997, 5½ x 8½, 168 pp, illustrated, soft cover.* **$13.95.**

☐ **14193 BACKYARD MEAT PRODUCTION, How To Grow All The Meat You Need In Your Own Backyard,** *by Anita Evangelista.* If you're tired of paying ever-soaring meat prices, and worried about unhealthy food additives and shoddy butchering techniques, then you should start raising small meat-producing animals at home! You needn't live in the country, as most urban areas allow for this practice. This book clearly explains how to raise rabbits, chickens, quail, pheasants, guineas, ducks, and mini-goats and –pigs for their meat and by-products, which can not only be consumed but can also be sold or bartered to specialized markets. Improve your diet while saving money and becoming more self-sufficient! *1997, 5½ x 8½, 136 pp, illustrated, soft cover.* **$14.95.**

More Titles of Interest:

☐ **17079 TRAVEL-TRAILER HOMESTEADING UNDER $5,000,** *by Brian D. Kelling, with Introduction by Bill Kaysing.* Tired of paying rent? Learn how a modest financial investment can enable you to place a travel-trailer or other RV on a suitable piece of land and make the necessary improvements for a comfortable home in which to live! This book covers the cost breakdown, tools needed, how to select the land and travel-trailer or RV, and how to install a septic system, as well as water, power (including solar panels), heat and refrigeration systems. *1995, 5½ x 8½, 80 pp, illustrated, indexed, soft cover.* **$8.00.**

☐ **14133 THE HYDROPONIC HOT HOUSE, Low-Cost, High-Yield Greenhouse Gardening,** *by James DeKorne.* An illustrated guide to alternative-energy greenhouse gardening. Includes directions for building several different greenhouses, practical advice on harnessing solar energy, and many hard-earned suggestions for increasing plant yield. This is the first easy-to-use guide to home hydroponics. *1992, 5½ x 8½, 178 pp, illustrated, soft cover.* **$16.95.**

☐ **14099 THE ART & SCIENCE OF DUMPSTER DIVING,** *by John Hoffman.* This book will show you how to get just about anything your want or need; food, clothing, furniture, building materials, entertainment, luxury goods, tools, toys — you name it — ABSOLUTELY FREE! Take a guided tour of America's back alleys where amazing wealth is carelessly discarded. Hoffman will show you where to find the good stuff, how to rescue it and how to use it. *1993, 8½ x 11, 152 pp, illustrated, soft cover.* **$14.95.**

☐ **13063 SURVIVAL BARTERING,** *by Duncan Long.* People barter for different reasons — to avoid taxes, obtain a better lifestyle, or just for fun. This book foresees a time when barter is a necessity. Three forms of barter; Getting good deals; Stockpiling for future bartering; Protecting yourself from rip-offs; And much more. Learning how to barter could be the best insurance you can find. *1986, 5½ x 8½, 56 pp, soft cover.* **$8.00.**

You can get these titles at your favorite bookstore, or contact any of our distributors, listed below:

Bookpeople
7900 Edgewater Drive
Oakland, CA 94621
1-800-999-4650

Homestead Books
6101 22nd Avenue NW
Seattle, WA 98107
1-800-426-6777

Ingram Book Company
One Ingram Blvd.
La Vergne, TN 37086-1986
1-800-937-8000

**Last Gasp of
San Francisco**
2948 20th St.
San Francisco, CA 94110
1-415-824-6636
Fax: 1-415-824-1836

Left Bank Distribution
1404 18th Avenue
Seattle, WA 98122
1-206-322-2868
jonkonnu@eskimo.com

Marginal Distribution
277 George Street N
Unit 102
Peterborough, Ontario
K9J 3G9
Canada
1-705-745-2326

Van Patten Publishing
19741 41st Avenue NE
Seattle, WA 98155
1-206-306-7187
Fax: 1-206-306-7188

Loompanics Unlimited
PO Box 1197
Port Townsend, WA
98368
1-800-380-2230
Fax: 1-360-385-7785